C000103859

Wristwatches

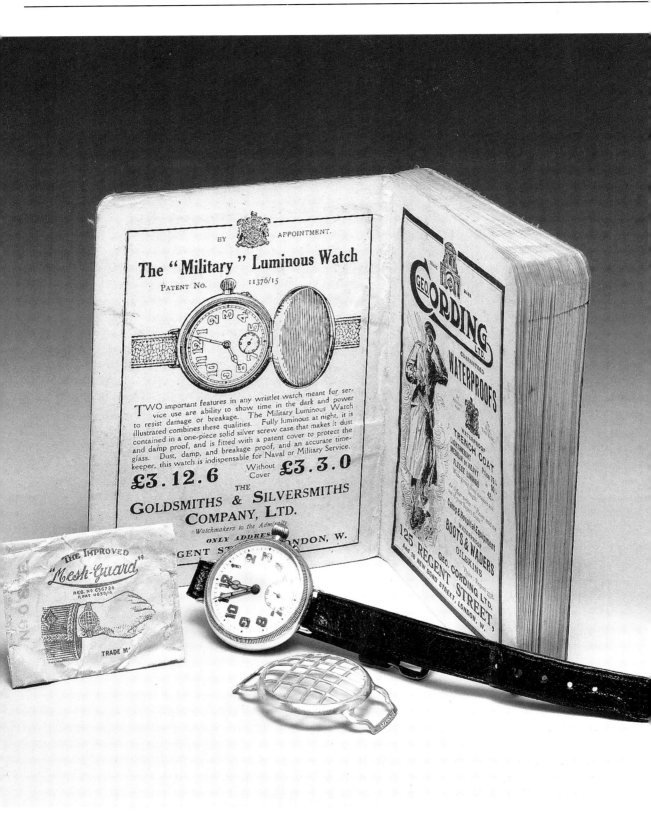

WRISTWATCHES
A Handbook and Price Guide
Revised 6th Edition

Gisbert L. Brunner & Christian Pfeiffer-Belli

Schiffer Publishing Ltd

4880 Lower Valley Road, Atglen, Pennsylvania 19310

Illustration on page 2:
The "Military" Luminous Watch 1918.
Silver. Luminous numerals.
Hand-setting via button near the 4.
15 jewels. Flat hairspring.
Bimetallic balance. Screwed two-piece case.
(Sothebys)

Translated from German by Dr. Edward Force,
Central Connecticut State University.

This book was originally published under the title,
Armbanduhren,
by Battenberg Verlag, Augsburg

Revised 6th Edition
Copyright © 1993, 1997, 2000, 2004, 2005, 2009 by Schiffer Publishing Ltd.
Library of Congress Control Number: 2009931645

All rights reserved. No part of this work may be reproduced or used in any form or by any means—graphic, electronic, or mechanical, including photocopying or information storage and retrieval systems—without written permission from the publisher.
The scanning, uploading and distribution of this book or any part thereof via the Internet or via any other means without the permission of the publisher is illegal and punishable by law. Please purchase only authorized editions and do not participate in or encourage the electronic piracy of copyrighted materials.
"Schiffer," "Schiffer Publishing Ltd. & Design," and the "Design of pen and inkwell" are registered trademarks of Schiffer Publishing Ltd.

ISBN: 978-0-7643-3313-2
Printed in China
1 2 3 4

Schiffer Books are available at special discounts for bulk purchases for sales promotions or premiums. Special editions, including personalized covers, corporate imprints, and excerpts can be created in large quantities for special needs. For more information contact the publisher:

Published by Schiffer Publishing Ltd.
4880 Lower Valley Road
Atglen, PA 19310
Phone: (610) 593-1777;
Fax: (610) 593-2002
E-mail: Info@schifferbooks.com

For the largest selection of fine reference books on this and related subjects, please visit our web site at: **www.schifferbooks.com**

We are always looking for people to write books on new and related subjects.

If you have an idea for a book please contact us at the above address.

This book may be purchased from the publisher. Include $5.00 for shipping. Please try your bookstore first. You may write for a free catalog.
In Europe, Schiffer books are distributed by
Bushwood Books
6 Marksbury Ave.
Kew Gardens
Surrey TW9 4JF England
Phone: 44 (0) 20 8392-8585;
Fax: 44 (0) 20 8392-9876
E-mail: info@bushwoodbooks.co.uk
Website: www.bushwoodbooks.co.uk

Thanks for shopping with us.
Kindest Regards, Customer Care

RETURNING GOODS

Please re-pack, in the original packaging if possible, and send back to us at the address below. **Caution!** Don't cover up the barcode (on original packaging) as it helps us to process your return.

We will email you when we have processed your return.
---✂--
PLEASE complete and include this section with your goods.

Your Name: _____

Your Order Number _____

Reason for return _____

Select: Refund my order ☐ **Replace my order** ☐

(Please note, if we are unable to replace the item it will be refunded.)

Return to:
---✂--

RETURNS
Unit 22, Horcott Industrial Estate
Horcott Road
FAIRFORD
GL7 4BX

Contents

The Cartier "Santos," in production as of 1911.

Introduction

Take a look at your left (or right) wrist and gaze upon your wristwatch. Is it ticking? If so, then you belong to the contemporary people who have a keen awareness of time, which the American psychologist Robert Levine has called the "heartbeat of culture."

Tempora mutandur, times change, and people change with them. Something has happened that just ten years ago was likely to have been consigned to the realm of fantasy - the mechanical wristwatch. Whether old or new, for some time they have been making a glorious comeback and competing more and more with the ultra-precise quartz chronometers for people's wrists. Once again, wristwatches with a soul are wanted in ever-growing numbers. These timepieces whose seconds hands deviate charmingly but comfortably from the "official" time transmitted on the airwaves by cesium time. These time pieces, always seconds from official time, do not make slaves of their owners.

The renaissance of the ticking timepiece for the wrist was brought on initially by a small group of enthusiasts who simply did not want to accept the idea that the future was supposed to belong to that production-line product, the quartz watch from the Far East. Instead, they insisted on their beloved gems of fine workmanship and, for lack of alternatives, finally turned to the wristwatches of older times.

If, as is believed by many, it was mainly the ladies who made known their preference for the wristwatch at the beginning of our century, the new passion for ticking timepieces since 1983 came principally from the men. The reason: The high-quality wristwatch is seen today as the man's piece of jewelry. It can be worn if one wishes, in plain sight, characterizes its wearer as a connoisseur, and is useful as well. It is a joy to wear, every glance at the dial affords pleasure and pride of ownership. In any case, one looks at the dial of the watch, even though usually unconsciously, more often than one looks in a mirror. And the ladies of our society soon lost their willingness to hide their "hedonistic" pleasure in wearing a watch. They demanded and received the appropriate decoration for their wrists, though they often wore men's watches.

The resulting boom made prices for collectors' items explode within a very short time. The sensational news of ever-higher record prices at auctions knew no end. Thus it became inevitable that the wristwatch moved more and more into the realm of those present-day people who never cared until then what kind of timepiece sat on their wrist and told the time. This new awareness, what with the short supply of well-preserved old wristwatches, resulted in their becoming rarer and thus more expensive all the time. Therefore a demand developed for new products of the traditional watchmaker's art. Today the old and new watches coexist in an almost miraculous symbiosis. Both have their enthusiastic and constantly growing flocks of devotees.

The greatest benefit from this unexpected development accrued to those areas of handicraft and industry that included most of the producers of mechanical wristwatches: the renowned watchmaking firms in the west Swiss watch centers of Geneva, LeLocle, La Chaux-de-Fonds, Bieland, in particular, Vallée-de-Joux, where more than ninety percent of all mechanical components for watches have been invented and produced.

At the beginning of the sixties, there still prevailed throughout that area a serious crisis referred to in many journals simply as "the Crisis." It came just a hundred years after a no less serious depression, known as the "American Crisis," had shaken the west Swiss watch industry. Further crisis followed at almost regular intervals. Spoiled by success and thinking in monopolistic terms, many watchmaking firms had become more and more oblivious to timely trends after World War II. They produced watches that simply ignored the times and were thus unsalable. Bankruptcy and large-scale unemployment were the order of the day. In view of the hopeless situation, many of the trained watchmakers had to be retrained for fine mechanics or electronics. An uncanny stillness spread through the area. The windows and facades of the buildings with the once-proud inscription, "Manufacture d'Horlogerie" looked more and more bleak as growing numbers of them stood empty.

Only at the beginning of the eighties was attention given again - at long last - to abilities thought to have been forgotten long ago, such as creativity and master craftsmanship, but also to unsurpassed experience and a centuries-old tradition of watchmaking. For that reason there is now a broad spectrum of mechanical wristwatches available, particularly in the realm of complicated mechanical models that would have been unthinkable earlier. The most modern technology, especially computer-controlled design and production methods, makes it possible.

What was lost in the process was the variety of previous years and decades in terms of the movements and their manufacturers. Hundreds of different caliber's with manual or automatic winding, with chronograph, alarm or other additional functions can be seen in the catalogs up to about 1970. They will never exist again, regardless of demand, for setting up assembly lines to produce them would drive the prices of raw movements to astronomic heights. This very situation makes it interesting and fascinating to collect wristwatches. This is true whether one collects one particular area, such as automatic watches, chronographs, alarm watches or chronometers, or across the board.

What is most important is that one should become involved in depth with the immensely broad spectrum of the wristwatch before one begins to collect. Only then can one avoid mistakes that can quickly cut into one's assets in this not-so-inexpensive hobby.

This book is especially intended to be of help in this way. It will attempt to set up price ranges for the various groups of wristwatches, from the simple models to the most complicated luxury items. An attempt will also be made to make this complex area understandable, illuminate the market situation and clarify the technical aspects of the wristwatch.

A Brief Chronology of the Wristwatch

The history of the wristwatch as we know it today goes much farther back than one might believe, for the principles of the wristwatch go back more than four hundred years.

Compared to that, though, the history of the production wristwatch in the broadest sense of the word is comparatively modest. It covers scarcely more than a century and a decade. And as the common man's timepiece that can claim to be a piece of human cultural history, it has all been developed in this century.

Even though wristwatches hold a significant position in the history of horology, their importance has been underestimated. For us to understand the real importance of the wristwatch, we must first understand its history. Then we can appreciate collecting them as a hobby.

An essential prerequisite for the birth of the wristwatch, or more appropriately, its forerunners, was the watchmakers' progress in terms of technology and handicraft. Technical developments such as the invention of the mainspring, made the portable clock possible. The perfection of the handicraft of matchmaking resulted in, among other things, the increasing miniaturization of watches.

The picture is unclear as to when the first mainspring "watch" was made, and we can only be exact to within decades. On the question of the first use of mainsprings in watches, one can only determine that it must have been in France in the late 15th century. The name of Peter Henlein of Nürnberg is always linked with the first pocket watch. A certain Johannes Cocleusim wrote of him in 1511, in the context of a Nürnberg description of the world, the "Cosmographia Pomponii Melae": "Finer things are invented every day. For example, Peter Henlein (names Peter Hele in the original text), still a young man, brings out works that even the most highly educated mathematicians admire, for out of a bit of iron he produces clocks equipped with many wheels, and however one may use them, they show and strike forty hours without any weights, even when they are carried in one's breast pocket or wallet." But Enrico Morpurgo's researches have led him to conclude that portable clocks already existed in Italy in 1475.

Whatever the truth may be, the turn from the 15th to the 16th century is in any case a significant point in time regarding the future of the wristwatch. In Blois in 1518 the watchmaker Julien Coudrey (1504-1530) is said to have made two daggers with small clocks built into their handles for Louis XI. In addition, Emperor Charles V is also mentioned in the history books of watchmaking. He had a fondness for mechanical devices and wore a ring that was decorated with a tiny watch. In 1542 the mathematician Ubaldi is said to have received a similar piece of jewelry as a gift.

In addition, there certainly must have been numerous other personalities who wore a personal timepiece on a ring but whose doing so was not noted in the chronicles.

The watch's path to the wrist was already marked by that time. According to what we know today, it took three more decades and led to the Queen of England: Queen Elizabeth I. In 1571, the year in which the Reformation was reintroduced, the Queen is said to have received the gift of a small watch fastened to a bracelet from her favorite, the Earl of Leicester. Here, at least according to what is known now, begins the history of the watch worn on the wrist.

The further course of this timepiece through the centuries can be listed in the table below for an easier overview:

1623 Blaise Pascal, a religious philosopher, mathematician and physicist later in life, as well as the inventor of the calculating machine, was born. It is said of him that he wore his pocket watch fastened to his wrist, and considering the rationalistic brilliance of this scientific genius, this cannot be denied.

1750 In the middle of the 18th century, according to numerous sources, it was very popular among mothers and nursemaids to fasten a pendant watch to a bracelet. In this position the watch was best protected from the hasty grasp of unpredictable children's hands.

1790 The "Schweizer Uhr" refers to a watch that was fastened to a bracelet, manufactured by Jaquet-Droz and Leschot and listed in their account books.

In both museums and private collections there are a whole series of wristwatches whose history can be traced back to the beginning of the 19th century, a time when the wristwatch was anything but a fashion article.

1806 The Parisian watchmaker and goldsmith Nitot, supplier to the court of the Emperor and Empress of France as well as the King and Queen of Westphalia, created two ornamental bracelets, one with a small watch, the other with a mechanically operated calendar. He made them on order from Empress Josephine, Napoleon Bonaparte's wife, who was accustomed to excessive luxury. She had ordered them as wedding presents for Amalie Auguste, a daughter of King Maximilian I of Bavaria, who was to marry Josephine's son from her first marriage, Prince Eugene.

1831 Until 1838 the House of Breguet delivered various small watches with armbands to various customers. Inside them, according to the manufacturer's archives, were eight-lignes movements.

1854 The horse bus was introduced in Paris. The drivers - or coachmen, as they might be called - were said to have worn wristwatches, presumably service watches, to keep their schedules.

1868 The Geneva firm of Patek Philippe & Co. began to produce a gold bracelet with built-in watch. It could only be put on the market five years later, in 1873.

1878 Wristwatches produced in small series in Vienna appeared on the market. The chroniclers say they were "worn by gentlemen for their own convenience."

1880 Around this time the first wristwatches presumably made in large series were produced. They were paid for by the German Navy, which had ordered them from the firm of Girard Perregaux in the watchmaking center of La Chaux-de-Fonds as service watches to be worn on the wrist. They were equipped with either ten-or twelve-lignes movements.

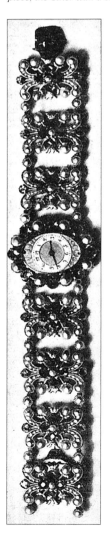

Two ornamental wristwatches by Nitot, one a timepiece, the other with a calendar, 1806.

The production wristwatches made their way from the wrists of gentlemen to those of ladies, and at first primarily in the form of jewelry. In technical terms, the series production of wristwatches would have been possible much earlier when one considers the great progress made in the realm of raw-movement production, precise manufacturing and resulting interchangeability of parts for assembly.

The fact that it did not happen surely cannot be ascribed primarily to the watch industry itself, which did not leave any lucrative possibility untried, considering the regularly occurring watch crisis. The responsibility lies rather with the conservative and patriarchal attitude of the men. Their tendency to accept the known and reject the new can be seen in retrospect as a hindrance for the earlier acceptance of the wristwatch.

The watch industry itself, which constantly raised the question of their acceptability, may serve as proof of this theory. In the Biedermeier era, for example, when men's trousers were cut very narrow, the watch industry reacted by producing very flat pocket watches that would fit as unobtrusively as possible into the trouser pocket.

The greater acceptance of production wristwatches during the following three decades is attributable mainly to the ladies. The men, chiefly than a marginal position during this era. Their watches, though, were quite spectacular and particularly relevant because they made decisive contributions to the technical progress of the wristwatch.

1886 According to a report in the Journal Suisse d'Horlogerie, gold and silver wristwatches with so-called sheer were sold in Lucerne to foreigners, particularly to women tourists from America. Cylinder movements by the "Kulm" firm of Frédéric Cuanillon of La Chaux-de-Funds and, as the journal reports, they achieved "a nice turnover."

1904 Omega published a large advertisement in the Leipziger Uhrmacherzeitung, portraying the experiences of a British artillery officer during the Boer War (1899-1902). He had reported that the wristwatch was an indispensable part of his field equipment and had withstood the extremes of heat and cold, heavy rain and constant sandstorms very well. There was another great advantage: Military men had found it very helpful, sometimes even a matter of life and death, to read the time by a quick look at their wrist instead of having to go to the trouble of pulling a pocket watch tediously out of their uniform.

1907 During a party at Maxim's in Paris, the Brazilian aviation pioneer, Alberto Santos-Dumont, told his friend Louis Cartier that when he sat at the controls of his aircraft he did not have the time "well under control" with his pocket watch. Cartier reacted promptly, and on November 12, 1907 Santos-Dumont was able to make his renowned 220-meter record flight in his aircraft while wearing a wristwatch designed especially for him. With this prototype of the "Santos," which was put on the market as of 1911 with movements by the firm of Jaeger. The wristwatch moved a giant step toward its freedom from pocket-watch design.

An early lady's wristwatch with shear band, made in Switzerland around 1910.

1909 The first wristwatches with chronographs were made.

1912 The first wristwatches with date indication by hands from the center post were offered.

1914 The magazine "Femina" questioned its readers as to the significance of the wristwatch. The 4350 responses that came in were evaluated. Of them, 3437 were "completely favorable" to the wristwatch, 480 readers had no definite preference, and only 433 preferred the pendant watch to the wrist-watch.

1915 The first waterproof wristwatches appeared on the scene. They were naturally also a result of the military needs of World War I, then raging in Central Europe.

1916 A venerable, experienced specialist/dealer declared that, despite all the shortcomings attributed to it, the wristwatch was in demand, and that one had to respect the taste of the public. All the same, he regarded the preference for the wristwatch as an error of feminine taste, as the wrist was surely the most unsuitable place to fasten a watch.
In addition, he complained about the poor performance of these timepieces. Yet he stated that this fault was not a very great one for the women's world that dominated the market, for women did not need to know the time to the exact second anyway. For men, on the other hand, only well-made watches with anchor escapement were worthy of consideration, for they generally kept good time. But alas, these watches had unfortunately not achieved wide-spread popularity, since for greater profit the manufacturers placed more emphasis on the decorative aspects and the quality of the case.

It must be noted that the early wristwatches were in fact usually equipped with small cylinder movements. These could be produced at low cost and thus offered the manufacturers more financial flexibility in terms of case production. Then too, the manner of wearing the wristwatch and the criticism of specialists on the subject did not exactly inspire the watch manufacturers to invest much in the production of movements. One manufacturer explained the situation: "We were accustomed to regard a precision watch as a delicate object. One put one's chronometer carefully into one's vest pocket and pulled it out to read the time *and* let one's friends, relatives and acquaintances admire the mechanism of this masterpiece."

1919 Inspired by the appearance of the armored combat first used by the British on September 15, 1916 in the renowned battle of the Somme under the nom-de-guerre of "tank," Louis Cartier created another important and trend-setting wristwatch model which he later named "Tank L.C." The first examples of this model were given to General John J. Pershing, commander of the American troops in France, and other high officers of the American armed forces. In 1919 the "Tank L.C." was officially put on the market.

On September 18, 1919, the pilot Roland Rohlfs and his airplane set a world record for altitude by reaching a height of 34,610 feet (10,550 meters). Accompanying him on his wrist was a waterproof "Depollier" wristwatch, which came through the event without trouble despite an outside temperature of -44 degrees Celsius.

1922 The Parisian watchmaker Léon Leroy made a small series of self-winding wristwatches for Sir David Salomons. Seven of these models were also fitted with a calendar movement.

1924 Leopold Reverchon in the journal "Der Uhrmacher": "Today it can be said that it (the wristwatch) has conquered the world. It is worn by the store clerk just as it is by the woman of the world. But is has won its greatest popularity in the middle classes."

1923 The Watchmaker John Harwood applied for patents in Germany, Switzerland and the USA for a self-winding watch he had developed.

1925 The first special book on the subject of the wristwatch was published. The author, watchmaker Bruno Hillmann, described the wristwatch in it as "...a very special variety of watch...that is as hard to handle with the pen at the writing desk as on the worktable," and he wished for nothing as fervently as that "the day of liberation of the watchmaker from the tyranny of the wristwatch would dawn."

1926 The Kulmbach merchant Hans Wilsdorf, founder of the "Rolex" brand, applied for a Swiss patent for a waterproof case with screwed-in crown, the well-known "Oyster" case.

1927 On October 7 the stenographer Mercedes Gleitze, wearing a Rolex Oyster on her wrist, swam the English Channel in 15 hours and 15 minutes. The watch suffered no damage in the process. On November 24 the title page of the London Daily Mail, bought by Wilsdorf for some 40,000 Swiss francs, proclaimed the success of his design.

1929 Series production of the self-winding "Harwood" began. It was halted in 1931 on account of the worldwide financial crisis.

1932 The Rolex firm once again stepped into the limelight. While other watchmaking firms were still experimenting with more or less unrefined self-winding systems, Hans Wilsdorf patented the first self-winding watch with a rotor turning without limit, though only in one direction. This was the birth of the automatic wristwatch with unlimited functioning.

1942 The raw-movement manufacturer, Felsa, aided the decline of the one-way, self-winding watch with his "Bidynator" system. With the help of a switching gear, both directions could be used to wind the mainspring.

Movement with automatic winding, Harwood, 1929.

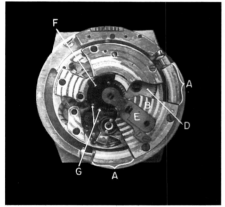

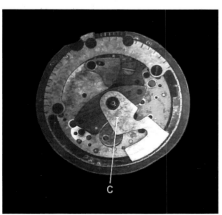

1946 Audemars Piguet put on the market what was then by far the flattest, hand-wound wristwatch, the caliber 2003. It is still in production today and measures 1.64 mm in height.

1948 The firm of Eterna introduced the first ball-bearing rotor in a self-winding watch. This form of rotor mounting is still the worldwide standard for good automatic wristwatches.

1969 On July 21 the first man set foot on the moon's surface. On his wrist he wore a Speedmaster-Chronograph with a hand-wound movement by Omega. In the same year, after long and intensive research, the first wrist chronograph with automatic winding could be presented to the eagerly waiting public. Competitors in the running for the privilege of being first were a work group made up of the Breitling, Büren, Hamilton and Heuer firms and the firm of Zenith. Both reached their goal at almost the same time, but in very different ways. Breitling & Co. settled on a movement in modular form, with winding by an integral micro-rotor. Zenith chose classical design principles with a central rotor.

At this time the first quartz wristwatches appeared, still large and expensive. But they were clear signals of the future trend. A few years later, when digital watches with multiple functions were offered at prices for which one could buy a simple mechanical "Timex," the worst crisis in the history of the Swiss watch industry was unavoidable, and the end of the mechanical wristwatch seemed to be close at hand.

1974 Switzerland still exported 11,653,514 movements and watches with automatic winding - a high point never again attained.

1978 Despite all problems, the Geneva designer Jean Lassale introduced the world's flattest mechanical watch movements: a hand-wound movement only 1.2 mm thick and an automatic caliber of 2.08 mm. Neither was to enjoy success on the market. On the contrary, after a short time the ambitious firm had to stop producing these movements and go out of business.

1980 For the first time, wristwatches in quantities worth mentioning appeared at major auctions.

1982 The classic wristwatch began to establish itself as a collector's item to be taken seriously.

1983 The first Swatch collection was introduced as the Swiss answer to the challenge from the Far East.

1985 In the process of the growing interest in old mechanical wristwatches, a renaissance of the mechanical wristwatch in present-day production also began.

Thus the wristwatch had finally attained that all-inclusive significance that should have belonged to it for many years as a result of its widespread popularity.

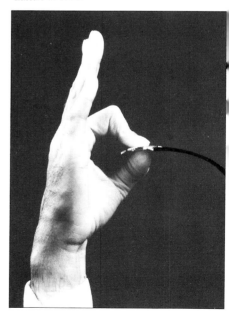

The world's thinnest wristwatch, made by Jean Lassale in 1978.

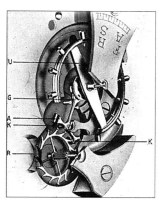

How Mechanical Clockwork Works

Depending on its design, a hand-wound movement is made up of 80 or more parts. It can be divided into eight important functioning groups:

1. The power system as its source of energy,
2. The transition system to carry the power to
3. The dividing system, also called escapement,
4. The regulatory system,
5. The system of hands,
6. The indicators of time,
7. The hand-setting system, and
8. The winding system.

By activating the ribbed winding crown (4), energy is conducted to the mainspring (18) via the winding stem (2) and the wheels and pinions of the winding system (12, 20). The larger of the two winding wheels (20) is connected to the mainspring arbor (21), to which the inner end of the mainspring is attached. The outer end of the mainspring is connected to the inner wall of the barrel. A ratchet (17) makes sure that the mainspring stays in its fixed coiled position.

After being wound, the mainspring is under pressure to unwind itself. It therefore creates torque against the center minute wheel (28) which rotates 360° once every hour.

The next or "Kleinboden" wheel (22) and the second wheel (23) conduct the energy further to the escape wheel (24). The gear train is planned so that the second wheel turns once per minute on its axis. In watches with a small second hand, the second hand is attached to the lengthened arbor of the second wheel.

The escapement, consisting of the escape wheel (**R**), the anchor with its pallets (**A, K**), the pallet fork (g), and the roller table and roller jewel (**R, E**) as well as the regulatory system, consisting of the balance (**U**) with its accompanying hairspring, utilize carefully regulated transmission to assure that the movements of the wheel train correspond to our measurement of time. This means nothing less than the extent of one second must correspond to the 86,400 part of a median solar day, or 9,192,631,770 oscillations in an atom of element cesium 133.

With what precision a watch approaches this ideal performance depends decisively on the quality of the escape system.

In the Swiss anchor escapement, the best escapement system found in wristwatches, the teeth of the anchor wheel slide on the cut surfaces of the ruby pallets of the anchor. With that, the anchor rod and fork are moved back and forth.

The fork of the pallets propels the roller jewel with it. Therefore the balance wheel moves by swinging in the same direction as the anchor fork. After the balance has swung to its extreme, the hairspring pulls it in the opposite direction. The roller jewel moves back into the cutout of the anchor fork and receives a new impulse in its momentary direction. The energy required for this is received by the anchor in the already described way, via the barrel and the wheel train.

The time elapsed for the balance wheel's oscillation depends on its inertia and on the active length of the hairspring as well as its elasticity.

Temperature variations, which are known to result in expansion or contraction of metals, can have a particular influence on the running of a watch. In order to reduce this, the thermion factors have to be compensated for. More information is included in the glossary under "bimetallic balance," "self-compensating hairspring," "balance" and "hairspring."

Another decisive factor in the precision of a wristwatch which is worn in varying positions is a balance ring that is balanced (weighted) as exactly as possible. In the so-called screw balances, this is done with the help of small regulating screws by which the moment of inertia can be changed. Modern balances are balanced by small borings in the ring. This is generally done electronically today. (See also "regulation" and "tourbillon" in the glossary.)

Ideally, the center of gravity of a balance should be exactly in the center of the balance arbor. This naturally applies to the hairspring too, which is connected to the balance arbor. In fine wristwatches, so-called Breguet hairsprings are used. Their raised outer end allows them to have a more concentric effect. In addition, it reduces possible center-of-gravity errors in the entire regulating system. In a simple manner, the swinging duration of the balance can be corrected by a change in the active length of the hairspring. For this purpose, a regulator is attached to the balance block so that it can turn. If the point of its indicator is turned toward **A** (advance) or **F**(fast), the hairspring is shortened and the watch runs faster. Movement in the direction of **R** (retard) or **S** (slow), on the other hand, makes the watch run more slowly.

So that one can read the time from a watch, the hand apparatus is also necessary. In reducing the turning of the minute wheel by 1/12, the hour hand, mounted on the quarter tube, thus makes one revolution on its axis in 12 hours.

Finally, the hand-setting system allows the hands to be set correctly to any time by turning the pulled-out crown.

In electric or electronic watches, the mechanical parts are more or less replaced by electric and/or electronic components. Their means of functioning can be seen in the following schematic drawings:

Four basic types of watches:

upper left:

the mechanical watch

(with manual or automatic winding)

upper right:

the electronic watch with balance wheel

lower left:

the electronic watch with tuning fork

lower right:

the electronic quartz watch

(with analog or digital indication)

Glossary of Important Wristwatch Terms

Adjustment: see "regulation."

Alarm: One of the earliest additional functions of mechanical wheel clocks is the alarm, which has been known since the 16th century. Wristwatches with alarms have existed since 1908, when Eterna patented such a model. The best-known production models are the Vulcain "Cricket," introduced in 1947; the "Memovox" by Jaeger-Le Coultre, introduced in 1951; and the Omega "Memomatic" of 1969.

Analog Time Indication: Time indication by a pair of hands that show the time by their positions to each other.

Anchor Escapement: see "escapement."

Anti-magnetic: "Unmagnetic" would be more correct. A watch is anti-magnetic when it is effectively shielded from the negative influences of magnetic fields on its running regularity.

Auto-compensating hairspring: Balance hairsprings made of spring steel have the characteristic of changing their elasticity with temperature changes. As a result, the running of the watch also changes. In order to counteract this, precision watches were equipped with a bimetallic balance until the thirties or forties of our century.
On the basis of extensive metallurgical research, a new type of balance hairspring could be introduced in the thirties. By being made of alloys of different metals, they were capable of counteracting temperature variations themselves. These self-compensating hairsprings first came on the market in 1933 under the name of "Nivarox." Because of their excellent characteristics, they found quick, widespread acceptance. The expensive bimetallic balance wheels thus became outdated.

Automatic Winding: The self-winding mechanical watch goes back to the year 1770 and the watchmaker Abraham Louis Perrelet. In order to counteract the frequent loss of the small key that was used for winding and hand-setting, Perrelet envisioned both a swinging pendulum mass and a rotor turning without limit. Their kinetic energy was utilized with the help of a special reduction gear to wind the mainspring. But since pocket watches experienced too little motion in the vest, trouser or jacket pocket, the self-winding system could not work effectively enough and thus did not go into general use.
Only the wristwatch, being attached to one of the most moving parts of the body, was suited to help automatic winding make its final breakthrough. The earliest model presently known, produced by the Parisian watchmaker Léon Leroy, came on the market in limited quantities in 1922. The first wristwatch with automatic winding to go into series production goes back to the Englishman John Harwood. Its design was submitted for a patent in 1923. Production began in Switzerland in 1929.

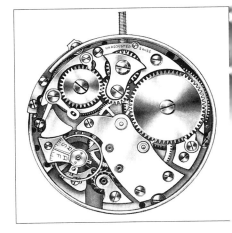

The movement of an alarm watch.

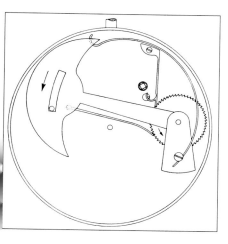

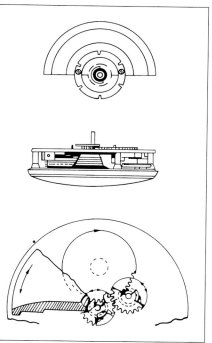

Automatic winding systems: above, with a swinging pendulum; below, with rotor.

In 1931 Rolex put the first wristwatch with a rotor winding system on the market. The mainspring was, to be sure, only wound in one direction. In 1942 the raw-movement manufacturer Felsa made the first switching system for adapting rotor energy. Thus winding in both directions was achieved. With the invention by Eterna in 1948 of the rotor mounted on ball bearings, all the requirements for future self-winding systems were in existence.

Aviation Wristwatches: Wristwatches that are designed and built especially for civilian or military pilots. The black or dark gray dial with large luminous numerals and vivid luminous hands. Among the best-known representatives of this genre are the "Mark **XI**" by **IWC**, the "**B**-Wristwatch" by A. Lange & Sons (Caliber 48.1, case diameter 55 mm, to be worn of the flight suit), or the corresponding models of **IWC**, Laco and Stowa.

Baguette Movement: A watch movement with a long rectangular form. By definition, the length has to be at least three times as great as the width. Baguette movements were particularly popular for wristwatches in the twenties and thirties. The smallest baguette ever, which is also the smallest mechanical watch movement in the world, was made by LeCoultre. It was introduced in 1929 and is still available. It measures 14 mm x 4.85 mm. It consists of 74 parts and weighs about one gram, dial included.

Balance: The balance wheel, in connection with the hairspring, is the organ that regulates the running of a mechanical watch. The precision of a timepiece depends very decisively on its design. The balance ring can be defined as a statically balanced "flywheel." In classic watch movements, the balance makes five half-swings per second, or 18,000 per hour, back and forth. In modern wristwatches, to increase regularity, the rate of the balance has been increased to 19,800, 21,600, 28,800 or even 36,000 oscillations per hour. Until the forties, bimetallic balance wheels were used in precision watches. They had a ring made of two metals with different heat-expansion co-efficients (usually steel and brass), soldered together. The temperature error of the simple steel hairspring was thus compensated for. When the self-compensating "Nivarox" hairspring was put into series production in 1933, the laboriously assembled bimetallic balance began to lose much of its importance. In its place, from 1935 on, more and more high-quality timepieces used the monometallic "Glucydur" balance rings, made of beryllium bronze. Combined with the "Nivarox" hairspring, this created an almost perfect regulatory organ that has lost none of its timeliness to this day. In watches of the medium price ranges and with standard movements, one often finds nickel balances of German silver, while simple pin lever and cylinder movements are usually fitted with inexpensive Roskopf balances of brass.

Balance-Stopping Apparatus: A device on a second stop watch which stops the balance while the watch is being set.

Bezel: A watchmaking term with several meanings. Strictly speaking, it is the glass ring of a watch case. This glass ring, with the watch glass pressed into it, is snapped into the middle of the case. Today turning rings that are attached to the front of watch cases to show various indications are often described as bezels.

Blind, Watches for the: Watches with particularly robust hands, in which the glass and its rim can be lifted up to allow the time to be read by touch.

Bridge: A specially formed metal part in which at least one pivot of a moving part of a watch turns. A bridge is screwed at both ends onto the plate, in which the bearings for the other end(s) are set. On the other hand, a potence is screwed down at only one end, while the other is free. Bridges and potences are normally named according to the moving parts mounted in them, i.e., minute wheel bridge, barrel bridge, balance potence, anchor-wheel potence, etc.

Cadrature: A name for the additional switching apparatus of complicated watches, such as the mechanism for a repeating watch or a calendar.

Caliber: Designation for the different movement types made by watch manufacturers. The caliber number allows the exact identification of a specific movement, such as for ordering spare parts.

Cap Jewel: A small disc-shaped synthetic ruby or actual jewel that is fastened over a hole jewel in order to limit the endshake of the arbor mounted in it. In wristwatches, the bearings of the balance arbor are generally equipped with cap jewels.

Central Second: A second hand located in the center of the dial. In watches with central second, the arbor of the minute wheel is bored out to make room for the arbor of the second hand. Watches with central second are divided into those with direct or indirect central second. The direct central second is part of the wheel train's power flow; the indirect is outside it. For that reason, indirect central seconds are often found in calibers that were rebuilt from decentral (small) to central second indication.

Chronograph: An additional function that allows a second hand to be started, stopped and set back to zero independently of the actual clockwork. The time indication is not influenced by it. Depending on their design, modern wrist chronographs may also have additional hands to indicate the number of full minutes and hours that have passed since the timing began.
The first wristwatches with chronograph were made around 1910. Self-winding wrist chronographs first came on the market in 1969.
Technically, the costly designs in which a so-called switching wheel serves to control the chronograph functions can be differentiated from the simpler types that use coulisse switching to control the process.

Chronograph, Split Second see "Split-second hand."

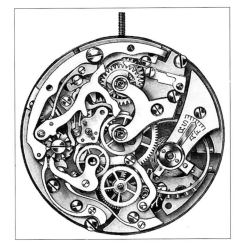

Chronograph movement with switching wheel

Complication: An additional mechanism in a watch. Among the most important complications of mechanical watches are automatic winding, chronographs, perpetual calendars, repeat mechanisms and alarms.

Crown: A knob for winding a watch, setting the hands and/or correcting the date indication.

Cylinder Escapement: This escapement system is no longer used in wristwatches today. It was invented by the English watchmaker George Graham in 1726. In this escapement there is no anchor to link the escape wheel and the balance arbor. Rather the teeth of the escape wheel mesh directly with those of the balance arbor; the latter has the form of a hollow cylinder. Because of its unsatisfactory running performance, the cylinder escapement was used chiefly in simple wristwatches.

Damascening: Decoration of the bridges and potences of a watch movement. The types include, among others, "large waves," "ribs" or a checkerboard pattern. After the cutting is done, the surface is gilt, silvered or rhodinized (rhodium-plated). The structure of the damascening remains visible through the surface plating. (see "Geneva stripes")

Date indication: Indication of the date, either in analog fashion by a hand or digitally by a disc. The hand or disc turns on its axis in 31 days. Every day at midnight it is switched one position farther via the hand system. When the date is shown by a hand, the numerals from 1 to 31 are printed on the dial. The point of the hand always points to the present date. Wristwatches with date indication by a hand have existed since about 1915. As of the midthirties they were largely replaced by watches with digital date indication through an aperture in the dial. These have the advantage of being easier to read.

All date indications in mechanical watches must be corrected for months with fewer than 31 days (see "perpetual calendar"). This is done in many watches via the crown and the hand system, that is, the hands are moved forward until the date is correct again. In modern designs, quick-correcting systems are used. Here either the hands must be moved back and forth between about 8:00 p.m. and midnight until the date is correct again, or the date can be set directly via the winding crown. For this purpose a medium position is used, into which the crown can be pulled. In a few wristwatch models there is a special corrector button set in the case rim.

Day Indication: Indication of the name of the present day. Like the date indication, this can be done by a hand or a disc.

Day indications do not usually need to be corrected, what with the regular rhythm of the weekdays. For that reason, only modern wristwatches offer the possibility of quick correction. Watches with day indication have been made since about 1915.

Cylinder escapement.

Under-the-dial view of a movement with simple calendar.

Digital Time Indication: The time is indicated by numbers. Mechanical wristwatches with digital time indication came onto the market in the mid-twenties. They had only small apertures in a closed all-metal case and were intended as alternatives to the "open" watches with crystal glasses, which was in common use at the time and extremely breakable. With the introduction of plastic crystals, mechanical wristwatches with digital time indication disappeared from the market. In the sixties they were offered again for a short time but did not become popular because the time was hard to read. Only with the electronic quartz wristwatch did digital time indication become popular. As of about 1975 this was done first with light-emission diodes (**LED**) which, because of their high electricity consumption, were soon replaced by liquid crystals (**LCD**).

Divers' Watches: see "waterproof wristwatches."

Duo-Dial Models: Watches with divided dials. Usually the hours and minutes are indicated in the upper half and the seconds in the lower half. The best-known representatives of this type are the Rolex "Prince" models, produced since the early thirties.

Ebauche: *Ebauche*, the French word for *raw movement*, forms the nucleus of the watch. It is the complete watchwork minus the escapement, balance, hairspring, mainspring, dial and hands. Ebauches can be bought from manufacturers in various stages of completion, such as with or without inserted hole jewels. Because of the expensive production facilities, they are developed and produced only by a few specialized firms.

Eight-Day Movement: A specially designed movement with a running duration of one week. Movements with one barrel are inherently different from those with two barrels in series.
Wristwatches with eight-day movements came into fashion in the twenties and thirties. The "Hebdomas" models are especially well known. They can be recognized clearly by a single large barrel which completely covers the back of the movement. The balance is usually visible through a cutout in the dial.

Electric Wristwatches: Wristwatches in which the balance is not powered by a spring but driven electrically. In the clockwork, as opposed to electronic watches, only conventional components such as spools, contacts, condensers or resistors are used. The balance of the electric watch is equipped with a contact. This closes and opens the electric circuit for a small magnetic spool. Its magnetic field is created by the balance through impulses of the required motion energy. Except for the fact that the battery eliminates winding, electric watches have no essential advantages over mechanical watches. After tuning fork devices were used, the running precision approached that of mechanical watches.
Electric wristwatches first came on the market in 1952. Notable manufacturers were Lip (France), Hamilton (USA), Epperlein (Germany) and Landeron (Switzerland).

Electronic Wristwatches: In the movements of electronic wristwatches there are both conventional components as well as semi-conductor elements such as transistors, diodes and integrated switches. In the world of electronic wristwatches there are transistor-controlled balance swingers (such as the Junghans "Datochron"), tuning-fork watches (such as the Bulova "Accutron") and quartz watches.

Escapement: The mechanism that transmits power from the mainspring via the wheel train to the balance wheel and its hairspring. The escapement consists of the escape wheel with its pinion, the anchor with its two pallets, the anchor rod with its fork, the safety rods and the balance wheel with its roller jewel and roller table.
In high-quality wristwatches, the Swiss anchor escapement is used almost without exception. The name comes from the specific form of the anchor developed in Switzerland and the geometry of the system. In the Swiss anchor escapement, the power is divided onto the pallets and the lifting surfaces of the teeth of the anchor wheel.
The escapement of a mechanical wristwatch does the hardest work: When the balance swings at a rate of 28,800 half-swings per hour, it makes the wheel train move forward 691,200 times within 24 hours. In the course of four years this adds up to more than a billion impulses of power that are passed on by the escapement. This represents approximately six times the work of a human heart.

Fly-back Indication: A hand moves to indicate, for example, the time or the date, along a segment of a circle (1 to 12 or 1 to 31) and then springs backward to its starting position when it reaches the end of the scale.

Formed Movements: Not round, but oval, pointed-oval, barrel-shaped rectangular or other movement shapes. Formed movements became more and more widespread at the turn of the century, in order to optimally use the limited space in wristwatch cases.

Four-Year Calendar: Unlike the perpetual calendar, the four-year calendar is able to show the varying lengths of the months correctly from one leap year to the next. It is always necessary to manually correct a watch with a four-year calendar on February 29.

Full Calendar: A complete calendar with day, date and month indication. The month indication is not switched automatically in any full calendars; sometimes it must be corrected manually at the end of the month. Unlike perpetual calendars, manual correction of the date and month indications in all months with fewer than 31 days is necessary here.

Geneva Seal: A seal of quality, with the Geneva city coat of arms, which according to a regulation made in 1886 is allowed to be affixed to such watches as "were shown by (official) testing to possess all the characteristics of quality work, run reliably, and include a minimum of work by artisans who live in the Canton of Geneva, as determined by the testing commission." This regulation was made considerably more stringent in 1957 by the formulation of eleven quality requirements that watches must fulfill to be marked with the Geneva Seal.

Geneva Stripes: Frequently used rib-like damascene decoration on the bridges and potences of fine watches. They are added before galvanization, but are still recognizable. (see "damascening")

Glasses: For wristwatches there are four different types of glasses: Crystal glasses are found mainly in early wristwatches. They are quite scratch-resistant but very breakable. At the beginning of the forties, crystal glasses were replaced more and more by plastic glasses (plexiglas). These are unbreakable, to be sure, but relatively easy to scratch. Mineral glasses have a hardness of 5 on the Mohs scale and are thus much more scratch-resistant than plastic. Sapphire glass is usually used in quality modern watches.
With a hardness of 9 on the Mohs scale, it is extremely scratch-resistant and shatterproof, and can only be worked with special diamond-tipped tools.

Gregorian Calendar: After long preparation, on October 15, 1582 a new calendar was put into effect by Pope Gregory XIII. It eliminated the small residual error of the Julian Calendar, introduced in 45 B.C. According to the latter, the year was 0.0078 days too long. For that reason, Pope Gregory XIII had sought ways to eliminate this excess time. His solution to the problem was to drop three leap-year days in four hundred years. Of the coming secular years (multiples of 100), from then on only those that could be divided by 400 would be leap years. Thus the year 2000 is a leap year, while 2100, 2200 and 2300 must do without the extra day. To compensate for the remaining residual error, leap-year day must be dropped again every 4000 years.

Hairspring: The hairspring can be called the "heart of the mechanical watch." Its inner end is attached to the balance arbor, its outer end to the balance bridge. Through its elasticity, it makes the balance swing back and forth evenly. Its active length, along with the inertial moment of the balance ring, determines the latter's oscillation rate. Therefore most watches include a regulator, which allows the active length of the hairspring to be changed. Lengthening the hairspring makes the watch run more slowly, while shortening it makes the watch run faster. The precision of a mechanical watch also depends on the shape of the hairspring. In high-quality timepieces, so-called Breguet hairsprings were formerly used. They have an outer end that is bent high up. Thus they can "unfold" more evenly than flat hairsprings.
The hairspring is three to four times thinner than a human hair and weights about 2/1000 of a gram. Yet it is capable of withstanding a tension of 600 grams. More than 200,000,000 times a year it pulls in its delicate windings and then stretches them out again.

Hallmarks: Information stamped into a watch case, stating, for example, the purity of the metal used or the karat, the country of origin, the year of manufacture, or the case manufacturer. The trade mark of the watchmaking firm, and a reference or serial number are also found frequently. (See the illustrations).

opposite, upper left: Swiss hallmarks.

opposite, lower left: French hallmarks.

opposite, upper right: French hallmarks.

opposite, right center: Hallmarks from Swiss cases made for export.

opposite, lower right: German gold and silver hallmarks.

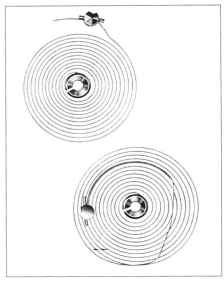

Hairsprings: above, a flat hairspring; below, a Bregu hairspring.

Golduhren

0,750	0,750-18K	18K-0,750
18K 0,750		72 18K 0,750
0,585	0,585-14K	14K-0,585
14K 0,585	9K 0,375	56 14K 0,585
0,375	0,375-9K	9K-0,375

Silberuhren

| 0,925 | 0,800 |

Platinuhren

| 0,950-PT | PT-0,950 | PT 0,950 |

Hallmarks for gold, silver and platinum cases.

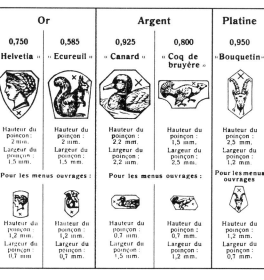

Or		Argent		Platine
0,750	0,585	0,925	0,800	0,950
« Helvetia »	« Ecureuil »	« Canard »	« Coq de bruyère »	« Bouquetin »
Hauteur du poinçon : 2 mm. Largeur du poinçon : 1,5 mm.	Hauteur du poinçon : 2 mm. Largeur du poinçon : 1,5 mm.	Hauteur du poinçon : 2,2 mm. Largeur du poinçon : 2,2 mm.	Hauteur du poinçon : 1,5 mm. Largeur du poinçon : 2,5 mm.	Hauteur du poinçon : 2,5 mm. Largeur du poinçon : 1,2 mm.
Pour les menus ouvrages :		Pour les menus ouvrages :		Pour les menus ouvrages
Hauteur du poinçon : 1,2 mm. Largeur du poinçon : 0,7 mm	Hauteur du poinçon : 1,2 mm. Largeur du poinçon : 0,7 mm.	Hauteur du poinçon : 0,7 mm. Largeur du poinçon : 1,5 mm.	Hauteur du poinçon : 0,7 mm. Largeur du poinçon : 1,2 mm.	Hauteur du poinçon : 1,2 mm. Largeur du poinçon : 0,7 mm.

POINÇONS SPÉCIAUX POUR L'ARGENT
(2 Titres : 950 et 800⁻⁻)

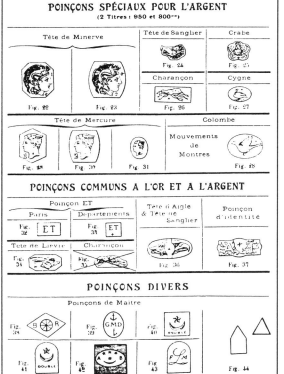

Tête de Minerve		Tête de Sanglier	Crabe
Fig. 22	Fig. 23	Fig. 24	Fig. 25
		Charançon	Cygne
		Fig. 26	Fig. 27

Tête de Mercure			Colombe
Fig. 29	Fig. 30	Fig. 31	Mouvements de Montres Fig. 28

POINÇONS COMMUNS A L'OR ET A L'ARGENT

Poinçon ET		Tête d'Aigle & Tête de Sanglier	Poinçon d'identité
Paris	Departements		
Fig. 32 ET	Fig. 33 ET	Fig. 36	Fig. 37
Tête de Lièvre	Charançon		
Fig. 34	Fig. 35		

POINÇONS DIVERS

Poinçons de Maitre

Fig. 38	Fig. 39	Fig. 40	
Fig. 41	Fig. 42	Fig. 43	Fig. 44

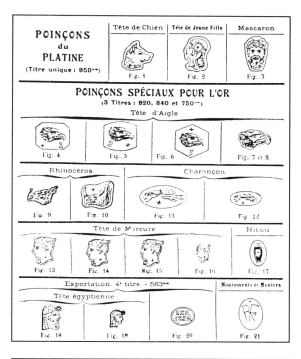

POINÇONS du PLATINE (Titre unique : 950⁻⁻)	Tête de Chien Fig. 1	Tête de Jeune Fille Fig. 2	Mascaron Fig. 3

POINÇONS SPÉCIAUX POUR L'OR
(3 Titres : 920, 840 et 750⁻⁻)

Tête d'Aigle			
Fig. 4	Fig. 5	Fig. 6	Fig. 7 et 8

Rhinocéros		Charançon	
Fig. 9	Fig. 10	Fig. 11	Fig. 12

Tête de Mercure			Hibou
Fig. 13	Fig. 14	Fig. 15	Fig. 16	Fig. 17

Exportation. 4ᵉ titre. - 583⁻⁻			Mouvements de Montres
Tête égyptienne			
Fig. 18	Fig. 19	Fig. 20	Fig. 21

Or		Argent		Platine
0,750	0,585	0,925	0,800	0,950
« Lynx 1 »	« Lynx 2 »	« Gentiane 1 »	« Gentiane 2 »	« Tête de lièvre »
Hauteur du Poinç : 2 mm. Largeur du poinç : 1,5 mm.	Hauteur du poinç : 2 mm. Largeur du poinç : 1,5 mm.	Hauteur du poinç : 2,5 mm. Largeur du poinç : 1,5 mm	Hauteur du poinç : 2,5 mm. Largeur du poinç : 1,5 mm	Hauteur du poinçon : 2,5 mm. Largeur du poinçon : 1,5 mm.
Pour les menus ouvrages :		Pour les menus ouvrages :		Pour les menus ouvrages :
Hauteur du poinç : 1,5 mm. Largeur du poinç : 0,7 mm.	Hauteur du poinç : 1,5 mm. Largeur du poinç : 0,7 mm.	Hauteur du poinç : 1,5 mm. Largeur du poinç : 0,7 mm.	Hauteur du poinç : 1,5 mm. Largeur du poinç : 0,7 mm.	Hauteur du poinçon : 1,5 mm. Largeur du poinçon : 0,7 mm.

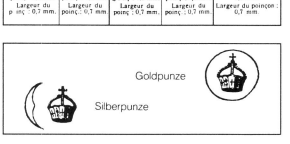

Goldpunze

Silberpunze

Hammer Automatic: Wristwatches in which the automatic winding is done by a swinging pendulum mass. Its movement is limited by buffer springs on each side.

Hand System: Located between the plate and the dial, it transmits the turning of the minute-wheel arbor to the hour hand. It also serves - in connection exactly with the pulled-out crown.

Hand-Wound Watches: Timepieces in which the mainspring must be wound by hand every day.

Heures Sautantes: Springing digital hour indication. Wristwatches with this feature came on the market in the mid-twenties. Instead of an hour hand, these watches have a disc under the dial, with the numbers 1 to 12. The present hour is shown digitally for sixty minutes through a window in the dial. As soon as the minute hand has reached the 12, the dial springs to the next numeral and thus moves one hour further.

Hole Jewel: A cylindrical synthetic jewel, today usually a ruby, with a hole bored in the middle. Hole jewels are pressed into the corresponding holes of the plate, bridges or potences to reduce friction and thus reduce wear. The fast-moving pivots of the wheel train turn in them.
In very high-quality watches, the holes in the hole jewels are slightly cone-shaped - the inner walls are gently rounded. This reduces the friction surfaces.
The hole jewels of fine watches used to be set in chatons and screwed to the plate, bridges or potences. This expensive form of attachment is no longer used today.

Jewels: To minimize the friction in the most important bearings, jewels are inserted on the anchor pallets and the ellipses of precision watches. Whereas natural gemstones (rubies or sapphires) were used in earlier times, only synthetically produced jewels are found in modern watches. They may be divided into bearing jewels (hole jewels), cap jewels, pallet jewels and roller jewels.
Many jewels used in a watch movement are not necessarily an indication of special quality. On the contrary: A high number of jewels noted on the dial of a low-priced wristwatch may suggest a high quality. But in these watches, the jewels are only rarely installed in the places where they are of real use.
A hand-wound precision needs at least fifteen functioning jewels: ten bearing jewels, two cap jewels for the balance, two pallet jewels for the anchor and one roller jewel for the ellipse. In complicated watches such as those with automatic winding, chronographs or repeat mechanisms, the number of jewels increases correspondingly.

An ultraflat automatic movement, 2.45 mm high; the rotor is made from a wafer thin slice of 21-karat gold.

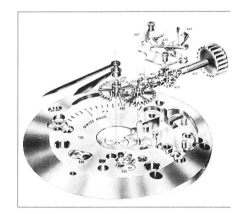

Under-the-dial view of a typical watch movement (with hands).

Karat: A measurement of gold content. Gold that is almost 100% pure has 24 karats. The case of an 18-karat gold wristwatch consists of 75/100 pure gold plus alloying metals (copper, brass, silver, etc.) 14-karat gold is 585/1000 pure, 8-karat gold 333/1000 pure, the remainder being alloying metals. The purity of a gold case is always stamped on.

Ligne: The traditional unit of measurement of the size of watch movements. It is derived from the French foot or "Pied du Roi." A ligne ('") corresponds to 2.2558 millimeters.

Mainspring: Mainsprings are long, elastic, spiral-shaped strips of steel that were already used as sources of energy in mechanical clocks in the 15th century. They are housed in a barrel and give their greatest torque when fully wound. As the spring's tension decreases, its torque also continues to decrease, which effects the running of the watch. In watches with automatic winding, the mainspring is rewound regularly. This results in relatively constant torque, and thus in more regular running. In general, "Nivaflex" mainsprings are used in wristwatches. They are made of a special alloy, and are durable elastic and very resistant to breakage.

Manufacturer: A watch factory that completely produces and finishes at least one caliber, producing the raw movement itself and putting it into a functioning condition.

Machanical Wheel Clocks: Clocks that are driven by a mainspring. The regulation of the running is done by a balance wheel with hairspring or by a pendulum.

A simple calendar with moon-phase device.

Moon-Phase Indication: Indication with the number of days since the last new moon. In the synodical month, one lunation, the time interval from new moon to new moon, or *moon phases* is exactly 29 days, 12 hours and 44 minutes. Such an indication usually consist of a disc with 59 teeth on its rim, and with two opposite full moons on its upper surface. Driven by the hour wheel, it turns once on its axis in two lunations. Its position is shown through a window in the dial. This cutout is sometimes complemented by a graduated scale of 29.5 days. Depending on their design, watches with moon-age indication can err from one minute to about eight hours in a year.

Moon Phases: The moon goes through its phases (new moon - first quarter - full moon - last quarter - new moon), which depend on the positions of the sun, moon and earth, in a lunation of approximately 29.5 days.

Pin Lever Escapement: Unlike the anchor escapement, the pin lever escapement has no pallet jewels in the anchor. Instead, vertically mounted hardened steel pins contact the teeth of the escape wheel. The "pin levers" became popular as of 1867 when the watchmaker Georg Friedrich Roskopf installed them in his low-priced pocket watches. It is still used today, though only in low-prices movements. The pin lever is robust, to be sure, but not especially precise.

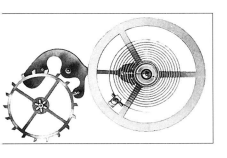

Rosskopf pin lever escapement.

Perpetual Calendar: A calendar system in which the different lengths of months in normal and leap years are adjusted automatically. Wristwatches with perpetual calendar usually include date, day and month indications. Various models also include leap-year indication.

The eternity of the watches with perpetual calendars manufactured to date extends only to February 28, 2100. Since that year has no 29th of February because of the nature of the Gregorian calendar, even perpetual calendars which show a leap year in their four-year pattern must be switched manually to March 1.

The perpetual calendar requires a complicated additional mechanism, which is usually mounted on the front plate and located under the dial.

Plate: Also called the movement plate. A metal plate that carries the bridges, potences and other components of a watch movement. The hand system is generally on the front side. The bridges and potences are fastened to the back.

In the plate are the threaded holes for the screws as well as holes for the bearings of the wheel train.

Potence: see "bridge."

Precision: A mechanical watch that shows a running deviation of 30 seconds per day (86,400 seconds) has a calculable quotient of error of 0.035%. Its grade of precision is thus 99.965%. At that, it far exceeds most mechanical machines.

Pulse Scale: A scale often found in chronographs as well as ordinary watches for doctors and nurses. Pulse scales exist in varying graduations, for 30, 20 or 15 pulse beats. The scale is always marked on the dial.

To measure the pulse rate of a patient, the chronograph is first started. When the indicated number of pulse beats is reached, the chronograph is stopped and the pulse rate per minute can be read directly from the scale.

Quartz Wristwatches: Electronic wristwatches in which oscillating quartz serves as a regulatory organ. The standard frequency of modern quartz movement is 32, 768 Hz, while quartz movements of the period around 1970 usually had frequencies below 10,000 Hz. (For example, the Swiss Beta 21 caliber, which went into production in 1969, had a quartz frequency of 8192 Hz.) Modern quartz watches generally show a precision of +/-1 minute per year.

One generally differentiates between quartz watches with analog or digital time indication.

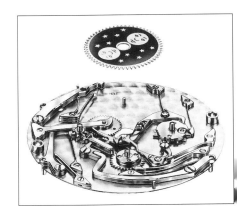

Movement of a perpetual calendar with moon-phase device.

Regulation: The regulation of a watch movement consists of observing and, if necessary, optimizing its daily running in various positions and temperatures. Depending on its quality and desired degree of precision, various types of regulation can be used. In the usual regulation of a good wristwatch, a test in two positions (dial up and pendant up) is made. The running deviations between these positions generally amounts to, at most, 30 seconds per day. In precision regulation according to official specifications, watch movements are tested in five positions and at temperatures of 4, 20 and 36 degrees Celsius. If this testing is undertaken by an officially recognized institution, and if a movement attains specified minimum values, then it may bear the designation of an "officially tested chronometer."
In every case, the prerequisite for optimal regulation is a balance wheel that is perfectly balanced. Otherwise changes in position will result in errors.
The art of regulating a mechanical watch consists in principle of keeping the frequency of the running regulator (balance and hairspring) as constant as possible despite external influences (temperature variation, position changes.) Deviations from the prescribed norm lead to running errors.

Regulator: An apparatus which allows one to make small adjustments for timekeeping.

Repeat Features: A costly additional function of a watch movement that allows the acoustic indication of the present time to be given to some accuracy. Depending on the design of the striking mechanism, one differentiates among watches with quarter-hour, eighth-hour (7.5 minutes), 5-minute or minute repeat. The latter form is the most complicated, most precise and most expensive of all. It must be able to indicate the time acoustically to the minute. While pocket watches with repeat features found broad acceptance, wristwatches with this complication have remained rare. They thus rank among the rarest collectors' items.

Running Reserve: The running time of a mechanical movement after being fully wound.

Second Stop: A device by which the movement and second hand can be stopped when the crown is pulled for hand-setting. The second stop allows the time to be set exactly to the second. For this purpose, the crown must be pulled out at the moment when the second hand is at the 12. When the time signal is heard, the crown is pushed in and the second hand goes into motion again.

BUREAUX SUISSES
DE CONTRÔLE OFFICIEL DE LA MARCHE DES CHRONOMÈTRES

Schweiz. Institute für offizielle Chronometerprüfungen
Swiss Institutes for official Chronometer tests   Oficinas suizas de control oficial de Cronómetros

Epreuves pour montres-bracelet - Prüfungen für Armbanduhren
Pruebas para relojes de pulsera - Trials for Wristlet-watches

Swiss made

Bulletin de marche / Gangschein / Boletín de marcha / Watch Rate Certificate	No	1838975	Mouvement / Werk / Máquina / Movement	No	6298

| Genre / Uhrenart / Género de reloj / Type of watch | B | Particularités / Besonderheiten / Particularidades / Watch specialities | s/c rem.main | Diamètre du mouvement mm / Werkdurchmesser mm / Diámetro de la máquina mm / Diam. of Movement mm | 26,0 | Hauteur mm / Höhe mm / Espesor mm / Thickness mm | 3,6 |

| Echappement / Hemmung / Escape / Escapement | ancre | Spiral / Spiralfeder / Espiral / Hairspring | autocompensateur | Balancier / Unruhe / Volante / Balance | monométallique |

S.A. Girard-Perregaux & Co
La Chaux-de-Fonds

Jours - Tage Dias - Days	Marches journalières Tägliche Gänge Marchas diarias Daily Rates	Variations des marches journalières Differenz der täglichen Gänge Diferencias de las marchas diarias Variations of the Daily Rates	Positions - Lagen - Posiciones - Positions		Températures Temperaturen Temperaturas Temperatures
1.	M₁ + 1		Verticale, 3 heures à gauche / Vertical, las 3 a la izquierda	Vertikal, 3 Uhr links / Vertical, 3 o'clock left	+ 20° C
2.	M₂ + 1	V₁ 0			"
3.	M₃ − 1		Verticale, 3 heures en haut / Vertical, las 3 arriba	Vertikal, 3 Uhr oben / Vertical, 3 o'clock up	"
4.	M₄ − 1	V₃ 0			"
5.	M₅ + 4		Verticale, 3 heures en bas / Vertical, las 3 abajo	Vertikal, 3 Uhr unten / Vertical, 3 o'clock down	"
6.	M₆ + 4	V₅ 0			"
7.	M₇ + 1		Horizontale, cadran en bas / Horizontal, esfera abajo	Horizontal, Zifferblatt unten / Horizontal, Dial down	"
8.	M₈ + 1	V₇ 0			"
9.	M₉ + 1		Horizontale, cadran en haut / Horizontal, esfera arriba	Horizontal, Zifferblatt oben / Horizontal, Dial up	"
10.	M₁₀ + 1	V₈ 0			"
11.	M₁₁ + 7		"	"	+ 4° C
12.	M₁₂ + 1		"	"	+ 20° C
13.	M₁₃ + 7		"	"	+ 36° C
14.	M₁₄ + 1		Verticale, 3 heures à gauche / Vertical, las 3 a la izquierda	Vertikal, 3 Uhr links / Vertical, 3 o'clock left	+ 20° C
15.	M₁₅ + 1		"	"	+ 20° C

Date de la fin des épreuves: **31 mars 1966**

Résultats - Ergebnisse - Resultados - Summary

Marche journalière moyenne dans les différentes positions / Mittlerer täglicher Gang in den verschiedenen Lagen / Marcha diaria media en las distintas posiciones / Mean daily rate in the different positions } **+ 1,2**

Plus grande différence entre la marche journalière moyenne et l'une des marches dans les 5 positions / Größte Differenz zwischen dem mittleren täglichen Gang und einem der Gänge / Máxima diferencia entre la marcha diaria media y una de las marchas en las cinco posiciones / Greatest difference between the mean daily rate and any individual rate } **2,8**

Variation moyenne / Mittlere Gangabweichung / Diferencia media / Mean variation } **0,0**

Variation par degré centigrade / Gangabweichung pro Grad Celsius / Diferencia por grado centígrado / Variation of rate per 1° centigrade } **0,0**

Plus grande variation / Größte Abweichung / Máxima diferencia / Maximum variation } **0,0**

Erreur secondaire / Sekundäre Kompensationsfehler / Error secundario / Secondary error } **0,0**

Différence du plat au pendu / Differenz zwischen liegend und hängend / Diferencia entre horizontal y vertical / Difference between flat and hanging positions } **0,0**

Reprise de marche / Wiederaufnahme des Ganges / Continuación de la marcha / Rate resuming } **0,0**

La Chaux-de-Fonds, le / den / el / the **31 mars** 19**66**

LE DIRECTEUR:

Tous les valeurs indiquées sont en secondes / Alle Werte sind in Sekunden ausgedrückt / The values are indicated in seconds / Todos los valores son expresados en segundos

Performance certificate for a wrist chronometer with hand-wound movement.

Skeleton movement.

Shock-Resistance or shock proofing: A system to protect the fine and sensitive pivots of the balance arbor from breakage. For this purpose, the hole and cap jewels of the balance-arbor bearings are attached to the plate and the balance potence with springs. They give way either laterally or axially under hard shocks.

A shock-resistant wristwatch is supposed to survive a fall, undamaged, onto a hardwood floor from a distance of one meter. In addition, it is not supposed to show any essential running deviation afterward.

Wristwatches with shock-resistance were introduced in the thirties. The best-known and certainly the most widespread shock-resistance system is called "Incabloc." It can be recognized easily by its lyre-shaped holding spring.

Skeletonized Movement: A movement with its plate, bridges, and potences cut-out by hand or machine to the extent that only the material necessary for functioning remains. In this way one can see through the movement. Wristwatches with skeleton movements have existed since the mid-thirties.

Split Second Hand: An additional second hand, located over the actual chronograph hand. It serves, for example, for clocking intermediate times, and can be stopped with the help of a special mechanism independently of the chronograph. Then, after the intermediate time has been read, the split second hand can be made to catch up with the chronograph hand. This process can be repeated as often as is wished. Zero-setting the split second hand independently of the chronograph hand is not possible.

Wristwatches with split second chronograph features came on the market around 1920. Because of the high technical demands and the resulting additional costs, they have not been able to become very widespread. For this reason they are very desirable collectors' items today.

Stainless Steel: An alloy of steel, nickel and chromium. This material is rust-free, resistant and anti-magnetic, but hard to work.

Swiss Anchor Escapement: see "escapement."

Swiss Made: Indication of origin on the dial and/or the movement of a Swiss wristwatch. A wristwatch may bear this inscription only if its movement was assembled, set into motion, regulated and tested by the manufacturer in Switzerland. In addition, at least 50% of the value of all its components (not counting the cost of assembly) must come from Swiss factories. Also, the watch must pass technical testing on the basis of the norms in force there.

Tachometer Scale: A popular scale on the dial of chronographs to indicate average speeds. This works as follows: The chronograph is started when passing a kilometer marker. As soon as the next marker is reached, the chronograph is stopped. The average speed traveled, in kilometers per hour, can now be read directly from the scale. There are also tachometer scales in miles for the British and American markets.

Telemeter Scale: A scale on the dials of chronographs to indicate distances. For example, the telemeter scale was used during the war to determine the distance of enemy troops by the sound of their gunfire. As soon as muzzle fire became visible, the chronograph was started. When the sound was heard, the chronograph was stopped. Now the distance of the gun could be read directly from the table.

Tourbillon: A design invented by Abraham Louis Breguet in 1795 and patented in 1801 to compensate for the center-of-gravity error in oscillations and the escapement systems of mechanical watches. In the tourbillon, the complete escapement system is located in a cage - as delicate a one as possible. This turns once around its axis in a definite time (usually one minute). In this way, the center-of-gravity errors in a watch in vertical position regularly cancel each other out. In a horizontal position, though, the tourbillon has no positive influence on running precision.

Trench Watches: Wristwatches with a protective grid, a spring lid or a leather capsule over the glass. As the name suggests, trench watches were produced after the turn of the century, primarily on the basis of military requirements because the crystal glasses were not able to stand hard use. But the trench watch also enjoyed great popularity among sportsmen.

Tuning-Fork Wristwatch: A wristwatch in which a tuning fork serves as a regulatory organ. Thanks to its frequency (ca. 300 Hz), a greater running regularity is achieved. The best-known and most outstanding model with a tuning fork is the Bulova "Accutron," which was announced in 1959 and put on the market in 1961. The guaranteed running precision was +/-one minute per month. Particularly in demand among collectors is the Bulova "Spaceview" model, in which the tuning fork can be seen through the glass.

Twenty-Four Hour Indication: Watches in which the hour hand turns once around its axis per day, directly the hours from 1 to 24 on the dial. This form of indication is rare because it is difficult for the owner to get used to using. Wristwatches with 24-hour indication were first produced during World War I, so that soldiers in bunkers could read the time and know whether it was day or night outside. In addition to watches with just this system, there are also those with two hour hands. One of them turns once around its axis in 12 hours, the other in 24. To be able to read a second zonal time (world time indication) directly from the dial, either an indicator is moved in one-hour steps, often by the crown, or a turning bezel with printed or engraved hourly markings is used to show the applicable time difference.

Up and Down Indicator: A special hand showing the running reserve of the watch. This indication was popular in wristwatches of the fifties, in order to show the functioning capability of automatic winding. Up and down indicators are extremely rare in hand-wound wristwatches.

Waterproof Wristwatches: Watches whose cases, in their original condition, will not let water in up to a given depth. For this purpose the case itself, the glass, the crown and any push-buttons have to be made according to special criteria. According to present norms, a wristwatch may be described as "waterproof" if it is resistant to sweat, drops of water, rain, or, when diving, to water at a depth of one meter for thirty minutes. If a waterproof wristwatch is built to higher standards, one can usually find the appropriate values engraved on the case, sometimes as testing pressure in the form of atmospheres (atm.), or as water depth in meters. For example, three atmospheres represent a pressure of 3 kilograms per square centimeter, or a water depth of 30 meters. More stringent criteria apply to divers' watches; they must be designed for daily use of at least one hour at a depth of 100 meters of water. Waterproof wristwatches should be checked for watertightness once a year, if possible.

Wheel Train: In a normal hand-wound watch, the wheel train consists of five wheel-pinion pairs. The teeth of the barrel mesh with the minute-wheel pinion. On the same arbor is the minute wheel, whose teeth mesh with those of the intermediate wheel. This wheel meshes with the pinion of the second wheel, and the second wheel itself meshes with the pinion of the escape wheel. Via the escape wheel and the rest of the escapement system, the power reaches the balance wheel, which is thus kept in motion.

World-Time Indication: The division of the earth into 24 time zones of 15 degrees of longitude each, starting from the Prime Meridian of Greenwich, resulted in the development of watches with world-time indication. They indicate two or more zonal times simultaneously. To achieve this, either two or more separate movements are housed in one case, or an additional mechanism allows the indication of various zonal times, generally varying from each other in multiples of one hour. Many possibilities are offered by the "heure universelle" models. Here the times in all 24 time zones can be read simultaneously. The names of important cities, representing each time zone, are engraved in a turning ring. A 24-hour ring driven by the clockwork shows the time of day or night in these time zones. The hours of the local times and the minutes of all time zones are indicated with the help of the centrally located pair of hands.

Important Watchmaking Firms

AUDEMARS PIGUET

Founded 1875-1882 by Jules Audemars and Edward Piguet; located in Le Brassus, Vallée de Joux, Switzerland; renowned manufacturer of luxury watches of highest quality, with all complications, (such as calendar watches, repeat mechanisms, chronographs - also with sweep hands, Heures Sautantes); still extensively owned by the founding families today. Despite their high quality, the watches of this brand are sometimes undervalued.
Price range from ca. $2200 - 175,000.

BAUME & MERCIER

Founded in Geneva in 1918 by W. Baume and P. Mercier. In 1965 Piaget acquired the majority of the stock; today the firm is owned by the Cartier Group. Manufacturer of wristwatches in the medium price range; collector interest is mainly in chronographs and classic models. The prices of wrist-watches by Baume & Mercier begins at about $275. Prices tend to remain around that level.

BLANCPAIN

Founded in Villeret, Western Switzerland, in 1735 by Jehan-Jacques Blancpain; one of the oldest watchmaking firms in the world. Blancpain produces luxury watches presently and is owned by the SMH firm of Le Brassus. Blancpain produced, among others, the "Harwood" for the French market, as well as the various "Rolls" models. Prices for older Blancpain models begin at about $350 and tend to remain at that level.

BREGUET

Founded in 1775 by Abraham-Louis Breguet, probably the most brilliant watchmaker of all time. Presently owned by Investcorp, with headquarters in Le Brassus, Vallée de Joux. Breguet made many important technical inventions, such as shock-resistance, the Breguet hairspring and the tourbillon. Older wristwatches, such as chronographs, calendar watches or classic hand-wound models by Breguet are relatively rare and thus usually bring firm prices, starting at about $3800.

BREITLING

Founded in La Chaux-de-Fonds in 1892 by G. Léon Breitling. Specialized from the beginning in chronographs that made the Breitling name famous all over the world. In 1979 the trademark was acquired by the Sicura firm. The business is located in Grenchen today. The various chronograph models (such as Premier, Chronomat, Navitimer, Cosmonaute, Duograph), the world-time "Unitime" watch, and various calendar watches are desirable collectors' items. Prices begin at about $600, with a tendacy toward higher prices for especially sought-after models.

Wrist chronograph by Blancpain, from the fifties.

CARTIER

The wristwatches known by the name of Cartier today are based chiefly on the creativity of designer Louis Cartier. He designed, among many others, such famous models as the "Santos" (1907), "Baignoire" (1912), "Tank" (1917), "Pasha" (1932) and "Vendôme" (1933). These models enjoy special popularity among collectors, with relatively stable prices beginning at about $1800. After a phase of being overvalued, especially extravagant chronographs, repeating or design watches, now show a tendency toward declining prices.

CORUM

Founded in La Chaux-de-Fonds in 1955 by Gaston Ries, Simone Ries and René Bannwart. This watch manufacturer is known chiefly for extraordinary case and dial designs; today it also includes wristwatches with complications in its offerings. Early designer watches include the "Golden Tube," "Longchamp," "Buckingham," "sans heures" and "Lionheart." On account of the comparatively modest age of the company, no firm collectors; market has formed. Prices begin at about $375 but are not uniform.

EBEL

The firm as founded in 1911; its name is an abbreviation for "Eugéne Blum et Lévy." Still owned by the family today, the firm began primarily to manufacture private-label watches with the contracting firms' names on the dial. There were also Ebel watches, which are comparatively rare. Only after the firm was taken over by Pierre-Alain Blum did its products become better known and more widespread. This has affected the prices of older models, which began around $325 and are generally firm, especially for unusual models such as chronographs or formed watches.

EBERHARD & CIE

Founded in 1887 by Georges Eberhard and headquartered in La Chaux-de-Fonds. Its best-known products are wristwatches with chronograph and sweep hand. The first wrist chronograph came on the market during World War I. The brand is especially popular among Italian collectors. This has its effect on prices, which are relatively high and quite firm.

ETERNA

Company founded in 1856 by Dr. Josef Girard and Urs Schild, the first watch factory in the town of Grenchen. Owned by the Swiss PCW Group since 1984. Eterna has made a name for itself particularly through the invention of the ball-bearing rotor for automatic watches in 1948. For that reason, the early Eterna-Matic models belong in every automatic watch collection. But the firm has also made interesting chronographs, alarm, calendar and formed watches. The price spectrum begins at about $200 and generally tends to be firm.

EXCELSIOR PARK

Founded at St. Imier in 1866 by Jules-Frédéric Jeanneret. Early specialist in chronographs, developing its own chronograph calibers for pocket and wristwatches, and known for them until the firm's liquidation in 1984. Wrist chronographs by Excelsior Park are relatively rare. Despite a good reputation, the firm's name has remained comparatively unknown, which has kept the prices, beginning around $350, relatively stable.

GIRARD-PERREGAUX

There are three founding years for this firm: 1791, 1856 and 1906. In 1791 the watchmakers Bautte and Mouliné founded a factory in Geneva to manufacture watches. In 1856 the watchmaker Constant Girard married Marie Perregaux and the unified firm of Girard-Perregaux came into being. In 1906 G.-P. acquired the earlier firm of Bautte and Mouliné. The firm is located in La Chaux-de-Fonds. G.-P. has always made a name for itself in the realm of wristwatches through its unique creativity. This also applies to the lower-priced Mimo range. Since the brand is relatively unknown, some of its watches are undervalued.

GLASHUTTE WRISTWATCHES

These include wristwatches by A. Lange & Söhne as well as those signed with the "Tutima" name. The most highly valued models, with a tendency to remain stable or rise slightly, are those made by A. Lange & Söhne. The oversize aviation watches made for the German Luftwaffe are outstanding; the prices fluctuate in the area above $1500. The most sought-after Tutima model is the aviation chronograph developed for the Luftwaffe in 1941, whose price is presently constant at over $1500. Also of interest are the rectangular wristwatches with the space-utilizing rectangular Caliber 58; their prices begin at about $350. Less in demand are the postware wristwatches of the Glashütter Uhrenbetriebe (GUB), available at prices from $125.

HEUER

Founded in Biel in 1864 by Edouard Heuer, this firm does business today as TAG-Heuer. Until its bankruptcy in the eighties, it was one of the greatest and most significant manufacturers of stopwatches and chronographs, producing, among others, chronographs to order for Rolex. Heuer also made itself a name in sporting time measurement. Wristwatches by Heuer are sometimes still undervalued and available at about $250, and tend to remain at that level.

IWC

From 1868 on, this firm had a very turbulent history, with many near-bankruptcies. The only notable watchmaking firm in German Switzerland, it is located in Schaffhausen and has been owned by the German tachometer manufacturer VDO since 1978. Its wristwatches with IWC's own calibers stand out particularly for their high quality workmanship. The most sought-after model is the legendary "Mark XI" pilot's wristwatch with anti-magnetic inner case; it has stimulated prices to rise above $1800. The earlier "Ingenieur" models are also desirable; made of steel, they are also priced over $1500. The price spectrum for IWC wristwatches in general starts at about $500, and the prices are generally stable.

Girard Perregaux advertisement from 1946.

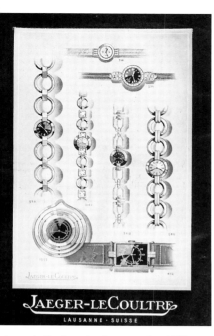

Jaeger-LeCoultre advertisement, circa 1940.

JAEGER-LECOULTRE

This watch factory in Le Sentier, Vallée de Joux, was founded by watchmaker Antoine LeCoultre in 1833. LeCoultre was and still is one of the most important manufacturers of ebauches, and has supplied almost all the notable producers of luxury watches. Until about 1925 the firm produced only ebauches. After its merger with the Alsatian watch factory of Edmond Jaeger in 1925, finished wristwatches with the Jaeger-LeCoultre signature also appeared on the market. One of the firm's best models, introduced in 1931, is the "Reverso," which brings prices starting at $2500 at this time. But the rectangular and round calendar watches the formed watches and the "Futurematic" with an up and down indicator, introduced in 1953, also bring stable prices starting at about $600.

JUNGHANS

One of Germany's most important and renowned watch manufacturers, it was founded in Schramberg in 1861 as a family business and is still located there. The firm is presently owned by the Diehl Group. Sought-after collectors' watches made by Junghans include the models with chronometer certificate, made as of 1952 with either manual or automatic winding (prices start at about $250 are quite stable); the "Minivox" alarm watch (prices start at about $200), and the chronographs with the firm's own Junghans Caliber J 88, special versions of which were made for the German Wehrmacht (prices start at about $600 and are likewise stable).

LE PHARE

Founded in Le Locle by Charles Barbezat in 1888, the firm has won many prizes and medals for significant inventions in the field of watch technology. In 1939 the firm moved to La Chaux-de-Fonds; in 1940 the brand was sold, and in 1950 it became Le Phare-Sultana S.A. It did much to attract business in the Far and Middle East. It is now the second largest Swiss manufacturer of chronographs. The brand is little known and thus undervalued; prices begin at about $200 and are generally stable.

LONGINES

The year 1832 can be regarded as that of the firm's origin; its founders were Auguste Agassiz and Ernest Francillon, the latter of whom bought the "Longines" or "long meadows" in St. Imier and built the first factory there. Longines has been able to make its name by developing outstanding calibers and inventing the so-called "Fadenriss" system for sporting events. Today the firm's legendary chronographs (prices begin at $1800 and are still rising) and the famous aviation watches of the "Lindbergh" type (prices from $5000 and quite stable) are most popular among collectors. Classic Longines wristwatches are available at prices starting at $300.

MINERVA

This firm was founded by Charles Robert at Villeret in 1858. In 1895 Minerva began to produce its own movements and cases. Wristwatches began to be produced around 1915, and the first Minerva chronograph caliber came onto the market in 1923. In 1934 the Haussener and Pelot families bought the firm, which has specialized since 1945 in chronographs, stopwatches and other measures of short times for various sporting events such as water polo and regattas. Since the firm is not particularly well known, its watches are sometimes undervalued. Prices for normal hand-wound models begin at $175, for chronographs at $600.

MOVADO

The Esperanto name of this firm means "always in motion." In 1881 Achille Ditesheim founded a watch factory in La Chaux-de-Fonds, which was given this name in 1906. The factory was already producing wristwatches shortly after the turn of the century. The "banana-shaped" Polyplan, with its arched movement (prices start at $2800) is especially desirable; it came onto the market in 1912. Also sought after are the calendar watches (such as the "Calendo-Matic"; prices start at $450) and the chronographs (prices start at $1500). Design devotees swear by the mechanical "Museum Watch" with the black dial, designed by Nathan Horwitt (prices start at $300). Prices tend to be stable or to rise slightly.

OMEGA

Among collectors, Omega is still one of the most renowned brands of watches. The firm was founded by Louis Brandt of Biel in 1848. In 1894 a new caliber bore the name of Omega for the first time. Today the brand belongs to the Swiss watch trust of SHM. The array of Omega wristwatches is very broad and extends from simple hand-wound watches to tourbillons. Among the more sought-after types are the hand-wound chronometers with Caliber 30 T2 (prices from $500) or the "Constellation" automatic chronometer introduced in 1952 (prices from $250). The chronographs, calendar watches and waterproof models with special cases are also very popular. Prices are usually stable.

PATEK PHILIPPE

This is almost a magic name among wristwatch collectors. The firm was founded at Geneva in 1839, linking the names of Antoine Norbert de Patek and Jean Adrien Philippe. The latter, by inventing the modern crown winding, contributed greatly to the everyday usefulness of the wristwatch. In 1932 the firm passed into the possession of the Stern family, but nothing else has changed to this day. Wristwatches made by Patek Philippe are valued very highly because of their high quality and the great demand for them; many models are even considerably overpriced. This fact has made itself known recently by heavily dropping prices for various wristwatches with complications. Prices dropping by 50% and more at many auctions have confirmed this trend. The price ranges of Patek Philippe wristwatches run from $2500 to $315,000.

Movado advertisement, circa 1940.

Patek Philippe advertisement from the forties.

ROLEX

Second only to Patek Philippe in fascination to the admirer of older wristwatches is the name of Rolex. According to a reliable source, the name is short for "horlogerie exquise"; it was registered by the German Hans Wilsdorf in 1908. The Rolex name is linked with the waterproof wristwatch, which was put on the market in 1927 under the name of "Oyster." Sought after by collectors are such models as the "Kanalschwimmer," "Bubble-Back", "Prince," and "Cosmograph," plus the chronograph models. Many fakes and knockoffs exist, and extreme caution is advised. Prices begin at $500, some are firm, while others tend to rise slightly.

ULYSSE NARDIN

Founded in Le Locle in 1846 by the watchmaker Ulysse Nardin, the firm has been owned since 1982 by Rolf W. Schnyder. Ulysse Nardin made a name for himself in the realm of precision time measurement with outstanding marine chronometers and observation watches. Collectors of older wristwatches prize the rectangular formed watches, chronographs and wrist chronometers above all others. Nardin has also made a few repeating wristwatches. The watches made by this firm are still somewhat undervalued; the prices begin at about $300 and are quite firm.

UNIVERSAL GENEVE

This watchmaking firm was founded, as the name suggests, in Geneva in 1894 by G. Perret and L. Berthoud. Its lower-priced brand is called "UWECO." Among collectors, Universal is best known by its various chronograph models (including the Compax, Tri-Compax, Dato-Compax, Aero-Compax). The firm's products also include simple hand-wound, automatic and calendar watches. In 1958 Universal introduced the microrotor, a planetary rotor mounted on the same plane as the movement. Prices begin at $500 and tend to be stable or rise slightly.

VACHERON & CONSTANTIN

This firm's products rank among the lesser-known and thus somewhat undervalued luxury watches. Founded in Geneva in 1755 by the watchmaker Jean-Marc Vacheron, who took in the wealthy Francois Constantin as his partner in 1819 for financial reasons. Today this watchmaking firm, still located in Geneva, is owned by Sheik Yamani. The products of Vacheron & Constantin includes both "normal" hand-wound and automatic models and wristwatches with almost every complication (such as chronographs, repeating, calendars). Prices begin at $1500; in the lower and medium ranges they are firm or rising slightly, while the upper and uppermost prices may be dropping.

ZENITH

This firm was founded in Le Locle in 1865 by Georges Favre-Jacot. During the course of the firm's history, more than 1500 observatory prizes, medals and other honors have been awarded to them. The name of Zenith was first used in 1911, when the original privately-owned firm was transformed into a stock company. In 1969 it was acquired by the "Mondia-Movado-Zenith" holding company, but it has been independent again since 1984. Despite its outstanding achievements in the field of the wrist chronometer and the design of the world's first wrist chronographs with automatic winding by a central rotor in 1969, the brand is relatively unknown and thus still undervalued. Prices begin at $300 and remain fairly firm, though they tend to rise slightly for various chronograph and chronometer models.

Zenith advertisement, circa 1964.

Collecting Wristwatches

It has only been for about ten years that wristwatches have appeared as a collecting area to any great extent. To be sure, there were collectors and admirers of mechanical watches before the "Wristwatch Fever" began around 1983; they collected interesting wristwatches in addition to pocket watches, which were long recognized as a collecting area, but there was only a small group and they inspired more amusement than admiration. Things were even worse for their few contemporaries who concentrated their energy solely on collecting wristwatches. In the eyes of "serious" collectors, they involved themselves with "second-rate" timepieces, objects that were once thrown into a corner in disregard or even thrown away when technology or fashion changed or when they could no longer keep when technology or fashion changed or when they could no longer keep reliable time and were not worth repairing. For that reason, wristwatches, as mere utensils, had no special value in the annals of human culture.

This is also shown by the fact that wristwatches - unlike pocket watches and large clocks - had no specific cultural-historical publication devoted to them until the early eighties. It did not seem worth the bother to publish books about the historical development and technical variety of wristwatches, as only a few people were interested in them. Only in repair manuals for watchmakers and in trade journals was the subject treated regularly.

Wristwatches were "everyday" objects and they were taken for granted, so no one gave any thought to their preservation. Technical innovations and fashion changed were accepted as facts, without reflection on the reasons for them.

On the other hand, the pocket watch enjoyed the respect given to an heirloom that undoubtedly possessed age, tradition, and at least abstract value.

Thus it was quite possible that, in some cases, less information was available on a typical twentieth-century product and its developmental history than on much older objects.

The situation has changed basically since then. A number of basic works provide information on the history and technical development of the wristwatch and make it possible to acquire a wide range of knowledge. In addition, there are special books about specific forms of the wristwatch as well as on the histories of renowned watchmaking firms. For the last few years a broad spectrum of special-interest magazines have also been available. Many of them are suitable, with the help of their text and illustrations, for contributing to one of the most important foundations for collecting: being informed, knowing what's what.

The collecting area of the wristwatch is a manifold and difficult one indeed. Hundreds of different movement calibers have been developed and used in many different brands of wristwatches over the years in Switzerland alone. For that reason, the name on the dial does not necessarily tell anything of the origin of the movement that is seeing service in the case. It helps to look in the so-called "Movement Seekers" that are published by the big spare-parts firms such as Flume and Essen. There are also great numbers of complications, including chronographs, calendar or repeating movements, alarms, world-time indication, and indications such as day, date, 24 hours, up and down indicator, and running times. They all require extensive knowledge if one does not want to regret the purchase of a collector's item after the fact. There is also the troubling fact that the wristwatch boom has also brought forth a variety of fakes and "marriages" (combinations of parts from different sources, not all original). (See the chapter on fakes)

Watches that are fakes or only partially original are worth much less than their original counterparts, and they are usually hard to resell, and then only at a lower price. Often, buying and consulting informative books can pay for itself even if one buys only one wristwatch.

The great variety in the types of collectors' wristwatches on the market also encourages one to reflect and decide what one would particularly like to collect. A collection can be limited, for example, to watches of one brand. It can also focus on specific complications, such as automatic winding systems, chronographs, chronometers, alarm, date or calendar watches. It can also be very interesting to concentrate on watches from one particular era, such as models made before 1930. Finally, collecting specific case forms also has its particular charm. Any kind of specialization surely brings its own reward because one soon gains knowledge and experience. It is safer to make a purchase then, rather than when one knows only a little about the subject. This also means that one does not face a crisis when one can afford only a few of the beautiful, interesting and/or practical wristwatches. Subjective reactions and spontaneous decisions to buy, such as while on vacation, can be safer then.

Another matter to consider is the financial appreciation of wristwatches; this is primarily of interest to those collectors who see the hobby chiefly as an investment. As with all other antiques, factors of fashion and economics, trends of the times, attitudes and reactions, and the resulting principle of supply and demand will prevail to determine the price level. Nobody can or will give a guarantee of a market development that will rise constantly. For that reason one is advised never to take up the collecting of wristwatches exclusive on speculation. Frustration and disappointment can enter the picture all too easily. When buying a wristwatch, the pleasure inherent in the object should always be in the foreground. Then the pain will be less severe if the value has not risen in the course of time as much as one may have hoped, or if a drop in prices has to be dealt with.

To put it briefly, the following five points should be considered when collecting wristwatches:

1. As thorough a knowledge as possible is of use in building up a collection or buying collectors' items. It helps to avoid wasting money when purchasing and investing.

This knowledge should include technical and historical as well as mercantile aspects. The study of catalogs from respected auction houses gives a particularly good overview of what wristwatches are on the market and their price ranges. The estimated prices stated in the catalogs offer only a general framework for orientation. Whether watches are actually sold for these prices can be determined only after an auction. For that reason, the lists of results published by many auction houses are an important completion of the corresponding catalogs.

Many specialist journals also report on the results of auctions, the trends to be seen in them, and the results of individual sales.

2. Specializing in a particular part of a collecting area such as the wristwatch gives the advantage of detailed knowledge and experience. Special situations are recognized all the more easily, and the chances of acquiring a rarity at a reasonable price are greater because one knows the true value of a particular watch.

In this respect it is helpful to be familiar with the types of movements used by the various manufacturers. A familiar or famous name on the dial is no indication of a caliber made by that firm, or of outstanding quality.

Watch manufacturers, troubled by numerous financial crises in America, Germany, Switzerland and France, sometimes had to make many compromises to survive.

In any case, though, one will have to pay considerably more for a wristwatch with a renowned, desirable name on the dial than for a similar model by an unknown maker, even if the same caliber is used inside it.

3. In the long run it is always worthwhile to pay attention to a good case, dial, and movement condition. The higher purchase price always means a greater lasting value.

The presence of the original packaging, original band and clasp always increase the value. Manufacturers of luxury watches, for example, often fit their leather-strap watches with buckles made of the same material as the case.

Compromises should be made when it is a question of obtaining a particularly striking and rare piece that is lacking in one's collection.

Every watch should be examined with a loupe before being purchased. A case knife can be handy to open snap-in case bottoms. To open screwed-in bottoms, on the other hand, one usually has to rely on the help of the seller or a watchmaker.

Most watchmakers, often to protect themselves from unjustified blame for damage, engrave their symbol on the case bottom after making repairs. Among other things, this also includes the date. Thus a careful look at the bottom of the case can usually tell something of a wristwatch's life story.

Screw-heads can also provide reliable information as to a watch's past. If work was done sloppily or with poor tools, the screw-heads are usually scratched and the slits are worn.

One should also have a good look at the dial and hands. If the dial is enameled, look for hairline cracks or blisters. A gleaming metal dial does not necessarily prove that the whole watch is in perfect condition. Such dials can be polished easily. But in the process they usually lose their original condition, even if the manufacturer's signature is reapplied. For that reason, one has to decide whether to give preference to a "freshened-up" dial or a somewhat faded but absolutely original one. One indication of "freshening up" can, but does not need to, be the absence of the lettering "SWISS" or "SWISS MADE" at the lower rim of the dial. The use of this lettering is limited by official restrictions. The same is true of the use of trade marks. Many manufacturers, such as Rolex, take action against any unauthorized use of their signatures.

The approval of the hands of a wristwatch calls for precise knowledge of what kinds of hands were traditionally used with certain dials. Old catalogs can be of help here. But it is usually easy to tell whether the hour, minute and second hands belong together. A critical look at their points can recognize false hands if they were cut down to the right size or are not the right length for the minute and hour markings.

4. When purchasing older wristwatches, one should put one's trust, when possible, in a reputable dealer or auction house. There are several reasons for this.

- As a rule, good dealers give a running guarantee, and offer repair service after it runs out. This is especially important today because qualified watchmakers who can and will handle wristwatches properly are not easy to find.

- Honest dealers are usually ready to provide a certificate of authenticity or at least write on the bill that the wristwatch they are selling is in original condition. If it should turn out after the purchase that the watch is not all original or faked, the watch would naturally be taken back and the purchase price returned.

- Serious auction houses also offer such services. Still in all, it is worthwhile to read the fine print of the auction conditions carefully. It will include information on the assurance of quality, the right to return merchandise and the responsibility to make good. It is always problematic when one cannot take the time to personally examine the goods in advance. In this case a knowledgeable and trusted person who can examine the goods thoroughly in advance is of great importance. The information given out by many auction houses as to the condition of the movement and case is always of a subjective nature and will not necessarily agree with one's own conceptions and standards.
For a price, usually 15% of the sale price, many dealers are willing to examine watches, estimate their values and bid on them within a previously agreed-on price range.

- Many dealers guarantee to take back wristwatches they have sold, at least at the sale price, when one later wishes to purchase a higher-priced item. Above all, one should always ask unknown dealers precisely about these and other guarantees and services. Those who are convinced of the quality of their wares will willingly agree to reasonable conditions, for satisfied customers come back or recommend them to others.

5. Joy and pleasure in a wristwatch should always take precedence over speculative value when buying. Only thus will the joy remain if, for whatever reasons, times change.

Wristwatch Preservation, Care and Repair

For the preservation of wristwatches, it is important to protect them carefully and maintain them regularly.

The following points should be kept in mind:

1. Wristwatches should be kept in as dry and dust-free an environment as possible. The cases should be separated from each other so that they cannot rub or scrape against each other. This causes scratches and signs of wear. Direct sunlight or other bright light should be avoided, as it can damage the dials and hands.

2. For insurance purposes, all the watches in a collection should be catalogued carefully. That means that one should photograph every watch and record its important data (manufacturer, year, type and complications, movement, case and reference numbers, as far as they are known, plus case material, condition, purchase price and seller).

3. If a wristwatch is put away for a long time after being worn, the case, and particularly the bottom, and a metal band if it has one, should be wiped carefully with a soft "Selvyt" cloth. The inevitably present traces of sweat, dirt, etc., will harm any case material in time.

4. If lying unused for a long time, waterproof cases should be tested for water-tightness by a properly equipped specialist firm. The materials used (usually rubber or plastic) chemically break down and can therefore unexpectedly leak when put into water, which can lead to expensive repairs. If such a thing should happen, it is time to take the watch to a watchmaker. Water has a deleterious effect on steel parts in a very short time. Surfaces attacked by rust can no longer be restored completely. Ugly traces of rust are always visible.

After using a waterproof watch in salt water, it is always advisable to rinse it off in clear tap water.

5. The oils used to lubricate the bearings and the escapement chemically break down, even if the watch does not run for a long time. This can become apparent if one winds the watch and it will not run, even though all the parts are intact. In this case the oil has hardened and become solid. It is also possible that the oil will flow away. The watch will still run, but the bearings are without lubrication, which causes excessive wear.

That is the reason for this basic rule for mechanical watches: The more regularly they are maintained and serviced by a qualified watchmaker, the longer they will last. As a rule of thumb, watches that are worn continually should be serviced every two to three years. To make this point clear, one can draw a parallel with an automobile: For a car that, on an average, only travels a few hours a day, the manufacturer prescribes a check-up, including an oil change, after the car covers a certain number of miles, or at least once a year. Almost every owner follows this advice, because his means of transportation is vital to him. On the other hand, a watch performs the hardest work - 24 hours a day and 365 days a year.

Despite regular care it can still happen that a wristwatch, for whatever reason, breaks down. Then a visit to the watchmaker is unavoidable. So as not to get the watch back in an even worse condition, one must choose a watchmaker carefully. It is advisable to consult friends, acquaintances or other collectors with similar experience.

Which types of repairs and servicing can be done to mechanical watch movements is shown in the following summary.

One must keep in mind that anything that goes beyond normal cleaning required you consider the availability of spare parts. To be sure, there are presently great numbers of highly qualified watchmakers who have specialized in the restoration of older watches. Many of them can make almost any part and even do major restorations. But since such undertakings consist for the most part of expensive handwork, one must consider the value of a watch first and relate this sensibly to the cost of repairs.

1. Cleaning a dirty or oil-hardened mechanical watch movement and then regulating it should be no problem for a competent watchmaker.

2. Replacing a broken mainspring, defective winding stem complete with crown, a broken lever spring, a click complete with its spring should be possible without any problems. These parts - at least for common calibers - should be readily obtainable from good parts dealers or the service department of the manufacturing firm.
    The situation is different in the case of very old or "exotic" calibers. In this situation, suitable spare parts will be found only in exceptional cases. For that reason, parts of similar size must be fitted, which should be successful when done carefully by a qualified servicing watchmaker.

3. The balance wheels of older wristwatches without shock resistance are problems of a very special kind. Their thin staffs break at a hard jolt. For common calibers, balance staffs can be obtained as spare parts. The making of a not directly obtainable balance staff requires experience and skill of a watchmaker, plus the necessary machines and tools.

4. For other parts, such as those of complicated movements like chronographs, alarms or automatic winding, the situation cannot be generalized. The watchmaker's concern and his connection with his parts dealer play a major role.

5. The restoring ("freshening up") of dials was already mentioned. As a rule, it presents no technical problems. But such an undertaking should be considered carefully in advance. It can change the look of a watch completely - the dial is, after all, a good 80% of what you see when you look at your watch - and cannot be undone. For that reason, it should only be considered as a last resort after a dial is completely messed up an all careful attempts to clean it have failed.

6. Hands can be replaced as a rule, but care must be taken to make sure the new hands match the dial and case in terms of style. The length must match too. Luminous hands are fairly easy to restore by filling with new luminous material.

7. Plastic watch glasses scratch very easily when a watch is subjected to hard use. They are available and replaceable in all sizes. This also applies to rectangular, square or other shapes. But at the time when waterproof watches were first being made, there were some 'adventurous' case designs with plexiglas cut especially to fit them. To what extent a replacement of this type is available is not certain.

The crystal glasses used until the forties do not scratch, but they do break very easily. Firms that specialize in them can replace them in the proper style if they have gone out of production.

8. Finally, scratched cases can be repolished by a skilled hand. This is considerably easier with cases of precious metals than with steel cases. Gilt, chromed or nickel-plated cases can be replated. In this case, though, polishing in advance is advisable.

Qualified case makers, gold - or silversmiths can still repair broken-off band attachments or defective hinges today. In looking for that special craftsman who is willing to spend extra time on a special project, consider winning his favor with your own kind words. If you fail, do not be discouraged; continue to look for a good craftsman. Even though this process is long and laborious, having your favorite or valuable wristwatch restored can be sufficient reward for your efforts. Do not give up too soon.

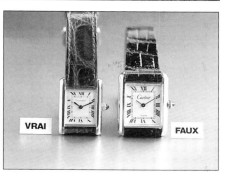

Above: destroying counterfeit Cartier wristwatches, Basel 1985.

Below: at left a genuine, at right a counterfeit "Tank" by Cartier.

Fakes, Knock-offs and Hybrids

Faking is as old as human art itself. It results from the efforts of unrenowned latecomers to bask in the sunshine of great masters and their works. But their plagiaristic efforts would never have been successful if there were not many people who, for whatever reasons, cannot or will not afford originals or, again for whatever reason, were not at the right place at the right time.

Things have not changed to this day. On the contrary, fakes and knock-offs enjoy ever-greater popularity, especially in the realm of luxury goods.

Since luxury wristwatches have developed into status symbols of the highest quality, the product pirates from the Far East and Italy present constantly growing competition. The fact that the manufacturers of the originals actively attempt to bring an end to this criminal activity has but little effect to stop the manufacture of knock-offs.

Knock-off wristwatches, especially of the Ebel, Cartier, Gucci, Movado or Rolex brands, flood the market. They can be found in the pushcarts of peddlers on Fifth Avenue in New York, in the street markets of Genoa or Naples, on the side streets of Kowloon or Bangkok. But one can also buy them in the quite average shops. The stock include almost exclusively copies of well-known brands with high market values. They are intended for those people who are willing to do without quality if they can get at least the appearance of an original for comparatively little money.

The manufacture and sale of knock-offs generally hurts only the actual owner of the brand name. The buyers are only in the rarest cases in the dark as to what they are buying. In addition, the degree of knowledge of the subject among consumers is relatively high.

The collectors of older wristwatches are only affected to a slight degree by this activity. What affects them is a very different category of falsification, done by those who can clearly be described as treacherous. Their intention consists of either directly imitating sought-after collectors' items or manipulating mechanical wristwatches so that they can be sold at a much higher price than they would have brought in their original condition. The spectrum of fakes has now become so broad that it can no longer be described and depicted without leaving gaps. Protection is offered only by caution, skepticism and restraint in buying presumed bargains, plus doing business with reliable dealers.

In this respect, special attention should be given to all sought-after models of major brands. Especially affected by the actions of falsifiers, to name only a few brands and models, are:

1. The Rolex Prince (Duo-Dial). After the same caliber was made for the Gruen Watch Co. by Aegler of Biel, it became quite easy to turn a reasonably priced Gruen into an expensive Rolex. This applies particularly to the striped gold "Prince Brancard" model or the "Prince" with springing hour indication at the 12.

2. The early automatic models by Rolex, called Bubble-Backs among collectors. The cases are fitted with hidden band attachments and are upgraded to pass as the sought-after "hooded" models.

3. The Rolex Oyster Chronographs. After similar chronographs were also marketed under the lower-priced "Tudor" brand name, these were soon disguised as the more expensive Rolex models. This done mainly by reworking the dials. The inside is ignored, since special tools are needed to open a firmly closed Oyster case.

4. The Rolex "Cosmograph" models with calendar and moon phases. By adding appropriate switching apparatus and modifying the case, normal Oyster models of the late forties and early fifties are turned into "Cosmographs."

5. The Cartier "Tank." Here gold cases are simply cast, dials printed and mounted on mechanical movements.

6. Cartier watches that are identical to the corresponding models by Jaeger-LeCoultre. The mere changing of the name on the dial can result in an extreme rise in the price.

7. Number 2441, the "Eiffel Tower," by Patek Philippe. It ranks among the most sought-after and expensive rectangular models by this firm. Here too, the case has been recast. To power the watch, a comparatively low-priced model with the required formed nine-ligne Caliber 90 is simply gutted.
Since Patek Philippe keeps the most detailed records of every watch the firm sells, a request to see the watch's ownership record may expose fakery fairly quickly.

8. Various models by Vacheron & Constantin. After a cooperative agreement was made in 1938, movements by Jaeger-LeCouptre were used in them. But the cases were also very much the same. The difference was the level of fine workmanship that was attained by Vacheron & Constantin. A Jaeger can be turned into a Vacheron fairly easily. If one does not take a careful look at the movement and the inside of the case, one may later regret it.

It has been considerably easier to create the many senseless faking of older wristwatches that have come onto the market of late. Even a collector who only deals marginally with the subject of wristwatches should realize that a watch with a signature of "Pateck Philippe" or "Patek Philip" cannot be genuine. A signature with a hyphenated "Patek-Philippe" was never used either. The presence of such an error should raise doubt in every case. Merely printing a well-known name on the dial of an inexpensive watch can be regarded as nothing but a clumsy attempt to take money out of ignorant, uninformed people's pockets.

On the other hand, it does not necessarily have to be a fraud if a wristwatch made by Audemars Piguet, for example, bears a familiar signature on the dial and the movement but not on the case. This can very well be an original watch. In order to avoid high import duties, many of the well-known Swiss watchmaking firms delivered only movements without dials until during the fifties, especially to the United States. There cases were made along the lines of the original designs, and the movements were mounted in them and regulated. In case of doubt, an inquiry to a manufacturer can be very helpful.

During the early years of our century, many well-known jewelers such as Tiffany, Gübelin, Golay Fils & Stahl or Bailey, Banks & Biddle, requested of their suppliers that the maker's name appear neither on the dial nor on the movement. Only the seller's signature was allowed. When one comes upon such a wristwatch, the high quality of the movement and the dial should catch the eye. Purchasing such a piece at a favorable price can be considered a very lucky incident.

When a wristwatch is composed of an old movement and a new case this is a form of fakery we call a "marriage." Such hybrids come into being chiefly because, in bad times, cases of precious metal were often melted down and sold for money with which to buy food. The remaining movements, sometimes of very high quality, were later installed in new cases. As long as the customer is informed of the state of things, there is no cause for complaint. But before buying such a hybrid, one must stop and think that though the price is well below that of an original model, the item will be very difficult to resell. Such pieces are scarcely suitable for speculative purposes.

Collector's Wristwatches and their Prices

An important reason why older wristwatches have caused such a stir in the past ten years is the tremendous rise of their prices. This basically applied to the whole spectrum of models, though it was particularly the products of outstanding manufacturers such as Cartier, Patek Philippe and Rolex that attracted special attention through the development of higher speculative prices in the world of auctions and dealers. This tendency for prices to rise, sometimes steeply, increased the popularity of other brands; as the demand for them grew, so did their prices.

The tempestuous developments in wristwatch prices must therefore be looked at from a variety of angles in order to become really understandable.

Unlike the collectors of large clocks and pocket watches, to whom one attributes more of an inner pleasure in collecting, an expanded knowledge, and a very collection-oriented approach to buying, the admirers of wristwatches are a very diverse group:

—First, there are the collectors in the truest sense of the word. They know their area of collecting very well and keep informed on what appears in the literature. Their purchases generally show that they are very aware of prices, which means they are usually not ready to pay any imaginable sum for a piece they lack. They proceed carefully in building up a collection and allow only good friends to see it. They wear an ordinary watch for every day use and keep the collectors' items strictly to look at and enjoy, and to wear on special occasions.

—Then there are numerous aficionados who buy fewer but very carefully chosen pieces with great enthusiasm. They place the highest value on watches with famous names and/or striking exteriors and they want to wear them. To acquire the watches they desire, they are quite ready to invest large sums of money, sometimes well over the market prices. Their buying behavior is often determined by emotion, sometimes because a certain detail of a wristwatch charms them because of its rarity or its fascinating decoration, etc. Even though it may seem irrational, it does not bother them to pay considerably more, for example, for a rare model with a black dial than for a more common model with a white dial - both, of course, made by the same manufacturer.

This group of collectors is also usually style-oriented. They like to seek out certain brands and/or models that are "in." Such buying practices cause prices to rise rapidly. Yet these people, as a rule, hang onto their watches tenaciously and part with them only when necessity forces them to. They usually read only the literature on their own realm, so as to know a lot about their favorite brands and models.

—Finally, in the corners of the wristwatch scene there are great numbers of speculators. The great historical, technical and craftsmanly achievements mean nothing to them, since dealing in wristwatches is just a quick and safe business. For that reason they buy primarily well-known brands and sought-after models and try to sell them again at a profit as soon as possible. In the catalogs of the great auction houses, wristwatches regularly appear that are put on the market repeatedly during a relatively short time. This can be confirmed by the printed serial numbers. In the years up to 1989, this trading was generally not very risky, and profits of 100% and more within six months were not at all rare.

Money plays only a minor role in purchasing when only good business is the goal. The knowledge of such speculators of the goods they deal in is usually limited to questions of what will sell.

The borders between these zones are, of course, naturally flexible. But this does contribute to the fact that setting prices in the realm of older wristwatches is very difficult and sometimes quite irrational. Concretely calculable factors like the quality of the workmanship, the complications or the age of a watch may give way partially to such aspects as rarity, origin, appearance and/or originality. In this context, the fact that the wristwatch has developed into a definite status symbol, especially in times of crisis, plays a role that is not to be underestimated. The chance of looking especially good wearing a certain wristwatch, of being noticed and envied for it, is very alluring. Naturally this also affects the price.

On the other hand, rather unimpressive looking wristwatches of the best origins, quality and condition are often much undervalued, on the principle that "what doesn't look good must not be good."

For that reason, the subsequent guide to prices should be regarded only as an attempt to make the market a bit easier to understand. They can and should not be regarded as dogma. The ups and downs of the market are simply too irrational for that. When gut reactions dictate prices, objectivity is lost. Thus caution is always advised, especially if wristwatches are to be bought primarily with the hope that their value will increase as much and as fast as possible.

The collecting of and interest in wristwatches is influenced to a high degree by developments in fashion and other related fields. And when the financial situation begins to get tight, people tend to save money where it hurts the least. This applies to wristwatches too, for in the end, one is enough to tell time by.

Panic sales in such situations can lead to a drop in prices within a short time. This was seen in 1990, 1991 and 1992 in the case of various highly overpriced luxury watches, namely those of Patek Philippe. After an unparalleled boom that climaxed in the 150th anniversary of the firm and a special auction conducted by the Geneva auction house (now antique dealership) of Habsburg, Feldman, the results of which were sensational, prices began to crumble. The reason can be seen in the probability that many of the watches in the price range above 100,000 Swiss francs were bought on speculation and/or with risk capital. Proof of this can be seen in the fact that a number of the watches, as the serial numbers show, were put up for sale again in subsequent major auctions in Basel, Geneva and New York. Insofar as their sales could be traced, their prices were considerably lower than before. It is worth noting that in the auction business the auction house receives a percentage from both the buyer and the seller. This varies from one auction house to another, but on an average it amounts to about ten percent.

For example, the world-time watch by Patek Philippe, #1415, with movement number 929572, cost around 244,000 Swiss francs at the special auction (all prices include fees). A year later, on April 21, 1990 it could only attract a bid of 170,000 Swiss francs at an auction in Basel, which was too low for the seller, for understandable reasons. In 1985 the same model was available for 22,500 Swiss francs, two years later for 63,000 and in 1988 for 82,500. On April 21, 1992 the price paid in Geneva for a #1415 with number 962773 was 110,000 Swiss francs, and one with number 964806 sold for only 93,500 Swiss francs.

A #1526 by Patek Philippe, a wristwatch with diamond-studded dial, stem wind, small second and perpetual calendar, number 967652, still cost 121,000 Swiss francs on October 14, 1990. On April 21, 1992 it was sold at an auction for 50,000 francs. With fees added, the resulting price is 55,000 Swiss francs. At the beginning of the eighties, the price level of this model was about 25,000 Swiss francs.

The price development of another outstanding wristwatch model shows the following curve:

Patek Philippe #1518

Price changes at Geneva auctions, in thousand Swiss francs, 1982-1992.

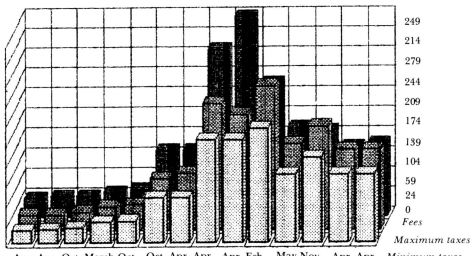

Unlike those of the high-priced wristwatches, the prices of collectors' watches have remained at least generally constant since their rise that culminated in 1990.

Since that time one of the most sought-after Breitling chronograph models, the "Premier" with a steel case, has sold for around $625 for three years. The Universal "Tri Compax," also with a steel case, has cost about $1550. The Rolex "Oyster Perpetual Bubble Back" in steel has sold for about $1250, the Bulova "Spaceview" with tuning-fork movement for $300, and the Jaeger-LeCoultre "Futurematic" in a 10-karat gold-filled case for $500.

The IWC cult watch, the so-called "Mark XI," has been able to continue its rise in value. Around 1985 it still could be purchased in silent auctions for about $100. Since then its price has risen to between $1500 and $1900.

From all of this, the following conclusions can be drawn:

1. Condition plays a decisive role in determining the value of a wristwatch, and strict attention should be paid to it. If it is ever offered for sale, its condition will be the first thing a potential buyer mentions as an argument for reducing the price.

2. The material is not always decisive in determining the price. If, for example, the steel version of a given model is rarer than the gold one, then the version with the steel case can be more expensive.

3. In Europe, gold bands (especially when soldered on) are scarcely taken into account. In fact, they can even have a negative effect on the selling price. For that reason, one should probably only purchase gold-band watches if one likes them personally.

4. The same is true of wristwatches with diamond-studded dials. Such items are sought after only in specific cases, such as rectangular art-deco models for the American market, certain Rolex models or ornamental watches for ladies. In classic watches, on the other hand, they rarely increase the value.

5. The dial is the most looked-at part of the watch. Therefore one should take a close look at the dial before buying. In addition one should not be too influenced by garish dial designs because unobtrusive designs take on the most classic look, and therefore endure the test of time.

6. Wristwatches are subject to fashionable trends. For that reason, the prices of specific models can drop very rapidly when the fashion changes. This has proved to be true, for example, for watches with moon-phase indication.

7. So-called "confirmation," and those with massive gold cases can never gain importance in terms of collectors' favor.

8. The prices of wristwatches generally vary from one country to another. This is related to the degree of familiarity of the brand name, individual taste and the degree of distribution that certain models have been able to achieve in a given country.

9. Some brands are chronically undervalued, while others, on account of the most varied factors, are relatively expensive. When one buys a "fashionable" brand of wristwatch, there is always a danger of paying too high a price.

Notes on the Prices in the Illustration Section:

The prices stated are carefully researched amounts. The relatively great disparity between prices are the results of the following conditions:

1. The prices are strongly dependent on the condition of the watch. Signs of wear, damage, non-original cases, dials or hands result, as a rule, in lower prices. A good-as-new condition, the presence of the original box, and papers can raise the price.

2. Many models were sold with a variety of cases, dials and hands. These factors can influence the prices strongly.

3. There are naturally large differences between the auction prices and the dealers' buying and selling prices. The dealer, like the final purchaser, has to be cautious when buying at auction, and when he resells a watch he has to get a margin of profit. The same applies to the difference between the price that one can get when selling a watch to a dealer and that which a buyer must pay the dealer for that watch.

The values are in U.S. dollars.

General Advice for Wristwatch Collectors

Auction Houses

The most important auction houses that include large quantities of wristwatches among their offerings are listed here in alphabetical order.

There are also a number of auction houses that also include wristwatches in general art auctions.

Information about auction dates and places can be found in the daily newspapers as well as the specialized journals.

Catalog subscriptions can be obtained from the addresses listed. Many auction houses send lists of auction results to subscribers and/or bidders after the auctions.

Antiquorum Auctioneers
2, rue du Mont-Blanc, CH 1211 Geneva, Switzerland
Auctions chiefly in Geneva, Hong Kong, New York

Christie's International
8 King Street, St. James, London SW1Y 6QT, England
Auctions chiefly in Geneva, London and New York

Dr. Crott, Stefan Muser, prop.
Postfach 120441, 68055 Mannheim
Auctions in Frankfurt am Main

Henry's Auktionen
An der Fohlenweide 30, D 6704 Mutterstadt, Germany
Auctions (jewelry and watches) in Mutterstadt; also reasonably priced collector's wristwatches

Auktionshaus Peter Ineichen
Badenerstrasse 71, CH 8026 Zürich, Switzerland
Auctions in Zürich

Auktionshaus P. Michael Kegelmann
Saalgasse 3, E 6000 Frankfurt am Main, Germany
Auctions in Frankfurt am Main

Auktionshaus Peter Klöter
Schloss Dätzingen, D 7403 Grafenau 2 (bei Sindelfingen), Germany
Auctions in Grafenau, also reasonably priced collectors' wristwatches

Bonhams
101 New Bond Street, London W1S 1SR, England
Auctions usually in the United Kingdom

Sotheby's
1334 York Avenue, New York, NY 10021
Watch auctions chiefly in Geneva, London and New York

Queen's Auktionshaus
Landsberger Strasse 146, D 8000 München 2, Germany
Auctions in Munich, with jewelry and reasonably priced collectors' wristwatches offered

Watch Markets

For some time, watch markets have been a standard means of marketing older pocket and wristwatches and clocks, applicable literature and tools.

They take place several times a year, presently in so many places that a complete list of them is neither possible nor practical. It is thus necessary to study the daily papers. The specialized journals also provide information in their calendars of coming events, or in the form of advertisements for the various markets.

One can gain information on what is new in the world of wristwatches at the "European Watch and Jewelry Fair," which takes place every April in the halls of the Baseler Mustermesse. The date can be found in the appropriate specialized journals.

Museums

See Christian Pfeiffer-Belli & Christoffer B. Konrad, Uhrenmuseen und Sammlungen historischer Zeitmesser, Munich 1992. It is unfortunate, but there is as yet no museum devoted to wristwatches. But wristwatches are already being exhibited in various museums within the realm of general clock and watch collections. Here too, it is not possible to give a complete list. Several important clock and watch museums are listed here:

Germany:

Deutsches Museum (German Museum), Clock Department
Munich

Uhrenmuseum (Clock Museum)
Furtwangen im Schwarzwald
(interesting wristwatch collection)

Wuppertaler Uhrenmuseum (Wuppertal Clock Museum)
Wuppertal-Elberfeld

Switzerland:

Internationales Uhrenmuseum (International Watch Museum)
La Chaux-de-Fonds
Uhrenmuseum "Château des Monts" (Watch Museum...)
Le Locle
(includes collection showing development of automatic winding)

Uhrenmuseum (Watch Museum)
Geneva

Patek Philippe Museum, Geneva.

Museum der Zeitmessung im Uhrengeschäft Beyer (Museum of Time Measurement in the Beyer Watch Company)
Bahnhofstrasse
Zürich

Plus various watchmaking company museums, such as Longines, Omega, Girard Perregeaux. (Rolex is opening in 2005)

Austria:
Uhrenmuseum der Stadt (Clock Museum of the City)
Vienna

Journals

They offer a very good overview of market happenings in the realm of old and new (wrist-) watches, offer announcements of and reports on auctions, calendars of coming events, and articles on watch history and technology.

In Germany:

Chronos
Ebner Verlag, Karlstrasse 41, D 7900 Ulm, Germany
(available at newsstands, 6 issues per year)

Klassik Uhren
Journal for Collectors of Classic Timepieces
Ebner Verlag, Karlstrasse 41, 89073 Ulm, Germany
(by subscription only, 6 issues per year)

Uhren Magazin, Riedstr. 25, 73760 Ostfildern, Germany

In United States:

Watch Time, Magazine of Fine Watches, 200 W. 57th St., Ste. 1410, New York, NY 10019

In Italy:

Orologi
Technimedia, via Carlo Perrier 9, I 00157 Rome, Italy
(available at newsstands, 12 issues per year)

Orologi da Polso
Edizion Studio Zeta, via S. Fruttuoso 10, I 20052 Monza, Italy
(only by subscription in Germany, 6 issues per year)

Orologi e non solo
Promoservice, via G.G. Porro 8, I 00197 Rome, Italy
(only by subscription in Italy, 12 issues per year)

Bibliography

Abeler, J., Ullstein Uhrenbuch, Frankfurt 1994.

Aebi, Peter, John Harwood, dedicated to the inventor of the automatic wristwatch, in Neue Uhrmacherzeitung, Vol. 5, 1966, pp. 18-20.

Audemars, Pierre, Louis Audemars - das Goldene Zeitalter, in Journal Suisse d'Horlogerie et de Bijouterie, 1954, pp. 151-155, 237-241, 301-305, 471-476, and 1955, pp. 93-95.

Audemars Piguet (ed.), La plus prestigieuse des signatures, special publication, Le Brassus, no date.

Baillie, G. H., Watchmakers & Clockmakers of the World, Vol. 1, new edition, London 1982.

Barracca, J., Negretti, G., & Nencini, F., Armbanduhren - die schönsten Sammlerstücke, Munich 1988.

————, Le Temps de Cartier, Munich 1989.

Berner, G. A., La montre-bracelet, autrefois, aujourd'hui, Biel 1945.

————, Praktische Notizen für den Uhrmacher, 3rd edition, Biel, no date.

————, Dictionaire Professionel illustré de l'Horlogerie, La Chaux-de-Fonds 1961.

Breguet, H., La boîte étanche, in Journal Suisse de l'Horlogerie et de Bijouterie, 1942, No. 2, pp. 65-68.

Breguet S. A. (ed), Breguet heute, Paris 1986.

Brunner, Gisbert L., Armbanduhren der Fabrikations-und Handelsmarke "Andreas Huber", Munich, in Uhren, 1982, No. 1, pp. 43-50.

————, Mechanische Armbandchronometer aus der Manufaktur von Junghans in Schramberg, in Alte Uhren, 1982, No. 4, pp. 312- 320.

————, Der Stundenwinkel-Armbanduhr Typ "Lindbergh" von Longines, in Uhren, 1983, No. 2, pp. 128-131.

———— & Sinn, H., Beobachtungsarmbanduhren - ein Vergleich, in Uhren, 1983, No. 3, pp. 243-246.

————, Armbanduhren mit ewigem Kalender, in Uhren, 1985, No. 4,
pp. 41-61.

————, Armbanduhren mit Repetitionsschlagwerk, in Uhren, 1986, No. 2, pp. 65-79, and 1986, No. 3, pp. 50-58.

————, Audemars Piguet - Manufacture d'Horlogerie, in Uhren, 1986, No. 4, pp. 9-40.

————, Breitling - Geschichte einer Uhrenmarke, in Uhren, 1987, No. 3, pp. 7-8.

————, Der Driva-Repeater, in Uhren, 1987, No. 3, pp. 68-69.

————, Blancpain - Uhrmacherei mit 250 jähriger Tradition, in Uhren, 1988, No. 1, pp. 9-28.

————, Eterna - 135 Jahre Präzisionsuhrmacherei, in Uhren, 1991, No. 5, pp. 33-48, and No. 6, pp. 9-24.

————, Das mechanische Uhrwerk - ein wunderbarer Mikrokosmos, in Die schönsten Uhren, 1991 edition, pp. 96-105.

————, Klassik Uhren Revue - Vorstellung alter, klassischer Armbanduhren, in der journal Chronos, 8 watches, since September 1992 (ca. 150 watches to date).

————, Der ewiger Kalender - Hommage an die Zeit, brochure for Audemars Piguet, Geneva-Bad Soden 1994.

————, Corum - die Leidenschaft für Design, La Chaux-de-Fonds 1993.

————, & Pfeiffer-Belli, Christian, Die Schweizer Armbanduhr, Munich 1990.

————, Pfeiffer-Belli, Christian, & Wehrli, Martin, Audemars Piguet, Munich 1992.

————, & Pfeiffer-Belli, Christian, Armbanduhren - von den Vorläufern bis zur Swatch, Battenberg Antiquitäten-Katalog, 2nd edition, Augsburg 1994.

————, & Pfeiffer-Belli, Christian, Klassische Armbanduhren von A-Z, Chronos-Buch, Ulm 1996.

Bureau de Documentation Industrielle (ed.), Einkaufsführer der Uhren-Industrie, Geneva, various annuals.

Calame, L.C. (ed.), Indicateur Suisse de l'Horlogerie, Biel, various annuals.

Cardinal, Catherine et al. (ed.), Der Mensch und die Zeit in der Schweiz 1921-1991, La Chaux-de-Fonds 1991.

Chaplay & Mottier S.A. (ed.), Annuaire de l'Horlogerie, Biel, various annuals.

Chapuis, A., & Jaquet, E., The History of the Self-Winding Watch 1770-1931, Geneva 1956.

Chaponnière, M.H., Le Chronographe et ses applications, Biel/Besançon 1924.

Château des Monts, Musée d'Horlogerie (ed.), Horamatic - Montres à remontage automatique de 1770 à 1978, Le Locle, no date.

Coboilli Gigli, N, Grazzini, G., & Gregato, G., Orologi-Storia, Costume, Collezionismo dell'Orologio da Polso, Milan 1986.

Cologni, F. & Mocchetti, E., Made by Cartier, Milan 1992.

Cologni, F., Begretti, G. & Nencini, F., Le Temps de Cartier, Munich 1989.

———, Piaget - Mythos einer Uhrenmarke, Munich 1995.

De Carle, Donald, Watch & Clock Encyclopedia, Reprint, New York 1977.

Dohrn-Van Rossum, G., Die Geschichte der Stunde, Munich 1992.

Ebauches S.A. (ed.), Les Ebauches - Zwei Jahrhunderte Uhrenindustrie, Neuchâtel 1953.

———, Technologisches Wörterbuch der Uhrbestandteile, 2nd edition, Neuchâtel 1953.

———, Répertoire des calibres classés par position tarifaire, grandeur et hauteur, Neuchâtel 1973.

Faber, E., Unger, S., with Blauer, E., Amerikanische Armbanduhren, Munich 1989.

Flume, Rudolf (ed.), Der Flume-Kleinuhr-Schlüssel K 2, Berlin/Essen 1963.

———, Der Flume-Kleinuhr-Schlüssel K 3, Berlin/Essen 1972.

Francillon, A., Histoire de la Fabrique des Longines, St. Imier 1947.

Fritz, M., Die Grande Complication von IWC, Schaffhausen 1991.

———, Reverso, die Legende lebt, Heidelberg 1992.

Girard-Perregaux (ed.), Horloger par vocation, La Chaux-de-Fonds 1991.

Gogler, A. S.A. (ed.), Indicateur Davoine - Indicateur Général de l'Horlogerie Suisse, La Chaux-de-Fonds, various annuals.

Gordon, George, Rolex, Hong Kong 1989.

Haider, R., Jacobs, O., & Zimmermann, A., Mechanische Armbandstoppuhren - Chronographen, Vienna 1988.

Hampel, H., Automatic Armbanduhren, Munich 1992.

———, Automatic Armbanduhren, Vol. 2, Munich 1996.

Hantz, Georges, Le bracelet extensible, in Journal Suisse d'Horlogerie, 1916, No. 1, pp. 1-4.

Harwood, John, Die Geschichte der automatischen Armbanduhr, erzählt von ihrem Erfinder, in Schweizerische

Uhrmacherzeitung, 1951, No. 11, pp. 31-34.

Herkner, Kurt, Glashütte und seine Uhren, Dormagen 1978.

———, Die Glashütter Armbanduhren bis 1945 von A. Lange & Söhne, in Schriften der Freunde alter Uhren, Ulm 1981, No. XX, pp. 125-129.

———, Urofa- und Tutima-Armbanduhren, in Schfirten der Freunde alter Uhren, Ulm 1982, No. XXI, pp. 81-85.

———, Glashütter Armbanduhren, Dormagen 1994-95.

Hillmann, Bruno, Die Armbanduhr - ihr Wesen und ihre Behandlung bei der Reparatur, Berlin 1925.

Huber, M., Banbery, A, with Brunner, G. L., Patek Philippe - Die Armbanduhren, 2nd ed., Geneva 1997.

Huber, Martin, Die Uhren von A. Lange & Söhne, Glashütte in Sachsen, 5th ed., Munich 1988.

Humbert, B., Die Schweizer Uhr mit automatischem Aufzug, Lausanne 1956.

———, Der Chronograph, La Conversion 1990.

Jaeger-Le Coultre (ed.), Die Uhrenmanufaktur, Pforzheim, no date.

Jaquet, E., & Chapuis, A., Technique and History of the Swiss Watch, London/New York 1970.

Jendritzki, Hans, Die Reparatur der Armbanduhr, 3rd ed., Halle/Saale 1944.

Jobin, A.-F., Klassifikation der schweizerischen Uhrwerke und Uhrenfurnituren, Geneva, ca. 1938.

Journal Suisse d'Horlogerie (ed.), Le Livre d'Or de l'Horlogerie, Geneva/Neuchâtel (1927).

Kahlert, Helmut, Die frühen Jahre der Armbanduhr, in Alte Uhren, 1981, No. 1, pp. 27-35.

———, Mühe, R., & Brunner, G. L., Armbanduhren - 100 Jahre Entwicklungsgeschichte (with price guide), 5th ed., Munich 1996.

Kocher, H., Die Geschichte der Uhrmacherei in Büren/Schweiz, Munich 1992.

Kreuzer, Anton, Die Uhr am Handgelenk, Klagenfurt 1982.

———, Die Armbanduhr, Klagenfurt 1983.

————, Faszinierende Welt der alten Armbanduhren, Klagenfurt 1985.

Lambelet, Carole, & Coen, Lorette, Die Welt von Vacheron Constantin, Lausanne 1992.

L'Associazione Piemontese Orafi e Orologiai (ed.), Elogio all'Orologio, Turin 1987.

Lavest, R., Grundlegende Kenntnisse der Uhrmacherei, 2nd ed., Biel (1945).

Les Fabricants Suisses d'Horlogerie (ed.), Les principaux types de chronographes expliqués par leurs cadrans, Biel/Neuchâtel 1952.

————, Offizielle Kataloge der Ersatzteile der Schweizer Uhr, Vol. M & O, La Chaux-de-Fonds 1948 & 1955.

Levenberg, Juri, Russische Armbanduhren (Vol. 1 & 2), Munich 1995.

Longines (ed.), Festschrift 1889-1989, St. Imier 1989.

Mann, Helmut, Porträt einer Taschenuhr, Munich 1981.

Manufacture des Montres Rolex (ed.), Hundertjahrfeier der Fabrik 1878-1978, Biel 1978.

Marozzi, Daria, & Tosella, G., Longines, Bologna 1990.

Martinek, Z., & Rehor, J., Mechanische Uhren, East Berlin 1981.

Meis, Reinhard, IWC-Uhren, Klagenfurt 1985.

————, Das Tourbillon, Munich 1993.

————, & Lang, G. R., Chronographen, Munich 1992.

Mercier, François, Mechanische Uhren mit automatischem Aufzug, in Alte Uhren, 1985, No. 1, pp. 21-32, & No. 2, pp. 27-47.

Montres Rolex S.A. (ed.), Rolex Jubiläum 1905-1920-1945, Geneva 1945.

————, Rolex Jubilee Vade Mecum, 4 Vol., Geneva 1946.

————, Un Jubilé Rolex, Geneva 1951.

————, The Anatomy of Time, Geneva, no date.

————, Hans Wilsdorf, Geneva 1960.

Nadelhoffer, Hans, Cartier—König der Juweliere, Juwelier der Könige, Herrsching 1984.

Negretti, G., & Nencini, F., Die schönsten Armbanduhren, Munich 1986.

Neher, F. L., Ein Jahrhundert Junghans, Schramberg 1961.

Odmark, Albert L. (ed.), Patents for Inventions, Class 139: Watches, Clocks and Other Timepieces, Vol. 2, 1901-1930, Seattle 1979.

Osterhausen, F. von, Chronometer Armbanduhren, Munich 1990.

————, Wie kaufe ich eine alte Armbanduhr, Munich 1993.

Patrizzi, Osvaldo, Rolex, Geneva 1993.

————, & Patrizzi, Madeleine, Collezionare Orologi Patek Philippe, Genoa 1994.

Pfeiffer-Belli, C., & Konrad, C. B., Uhren-Museen und Sammlungen historischer Zeitmesser, Munich 1992.

Richter, Benno, Breitling - Die Geschichte einer grossen Uhrenmarke, Munich 1992.

Schmeltzer, Bernhard, Wie alt ist meine Taschen-oder Armbanduhr, Duisburg 1986.

————, Die automatische Armbanduhr, Duisburg 1992.

Stolberg, Lukas, Lexikon der Taschenuhr, Klagenfurt 1983.

Swiss Watch Chamber of Commerce (ed.), The Inside Story of the Swiss Watch, La Chaux-de-Fonds, no date.

Tölke, Hans-F., & King, Jürgen, International Watch Co., Schaffhausen, Zürich 1986.

Vacheron & Constantin (ed.), In Genf seit 1755, Geneva 1973.

Viola, Gerald, & Brunner, Gisbert L., Zeit in Gold, Munich 1988.

Vogel, Horand, Uhren von Patek Philippe, Düsseldorf 1980.

Zagoory, J., & Chan, H., A Time to Watch, Hong Kong 1985.

————, The Movado History, Munchen 1996.

Zemanek, H., Kalender und Chronologie, Munich 1987.

Der Wassertropfen in der wasserdichten Uhr, in Deutsche Uhrmacher-Zeitung, 1943, pp. 148-150.

Exposition nationale suisse à Berne en 1914, in Journal Suisse d'Horlogerie, 1915, No. 6, pp. 179ff, & No. 9, pp. 242ff.

L'Accord Jaeger-LeCoultre - Vacheron & Constantin, in Journal Suisse d'Horlogerie et de Bijouterie, 1938, No. 9-10, pp. 155-159.

La montre étanche, in Journal Suisse d'Horlogerie et de Bijouterie, 1940, No. 7-10, pp. 177ff.

Les Origines des Montres-bracelets et des bagues-montres, in Journal Suisse d'Horlogerie et de Bijouterie, 1932, No. 9, pp. 185-189.

Rund um die Wasserdichte Uhr, in Deutsche Uhrmacher-Zeitung, 1943, No. 11-12, pp. 47-51.

As well as numerous firms' catalogues and advertisements, and the issues of the Journal Suisse d'Horlogerie et de Bijouterie since 1876.

Color Illustrations

1

F 2

F 3

F 4

F1 Patek Philippe (previous page)

Fifties, world time, 18-karat yellow gold. Special feature: enameled center with map of USA. Stem wind, Caliber 12-400. 18 jewels. Breguet hairspring. Monometallic screw balance. Shock resistance. The crown by the 3 is for hand-setting and adjusting the 24-hour ring, the crown by the 9 matches the ring with the place name.
(Habsburg) $990,000-1,080,000

F2

Round gold Swiss wristwatches of the fifties, with an alarm watch at right.

F3

Square and rectangular US and Swiss watches from the forties and fifties.

F4

Round watches from the early twenties. Silver and 9-karat gold. Special feature: protective grid and hunting case. Stem-wind. Swiss caliber. 15 jewels. Flat or Berguet hairspring. Bimetallic balance. Enameled dials.
(Privately owned) $360-720

F5 Cartier Chronograph

Thirties. 18-karat yellow gold. Stem-wind. LeCoultre caliber made for European Watch Co., 11 lignes. 25 jewels. Breguet hairspring. Bimetallic balance. 30-minute counter. All functions via the crown.
(Christies) $72,000-90,000

F 5 A

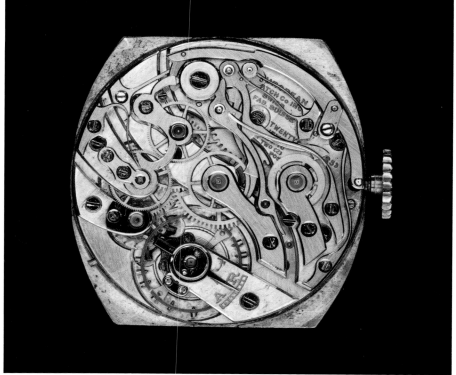

F 5 B

F 6

F 7

F 8

F 9

F6 Wittnauer Calendar Watch
Gold-plated. Rotor-wound. 17 jewels. Self-compensating flat hairspring. Monometallic balance. Shock resistance. Combination calendar through various scales to year 2020. Hand-setting crown by the 4.
(Breitsprecher) $270-540

F7 Patek Philippe
Circa 1953. Perpetual calendar with moon phases. 18-karat yellow gold case is stem wound. Caliber 27 SC. 18 jewels. Breguet hairspring. Monometallic screw balance. Shock resistance. Direct central second.
(Patek) $81,000-99,000

F8 Omega Flightmaster Chronograph
1976. Stainless steel. Waterproof screwed bottom. Stem-wind. Glucydur balance. Incabloc shock resistance. Two-zone time, turning minute scale. 30-minute and 12-hour counters.
(Breitsprecher) $720-1,080

F9 "Chevrolet"
1927. Steel. Watch in form of a Chevrolet auto radiator grille. Stem-wind. Movement by H. Didisheim, Switzerland. Caliber 2 C2. 6 jewels. Flat hairspring.
(Joseph) $720-900

F10 Glycine
1931. Barrel-shaped metal case. Automatic wind by oscillating pendulum. Crown only for hand-setting. Caliber 20.
(Privately owned) $720-900

F10 A–C

F 11

F 12

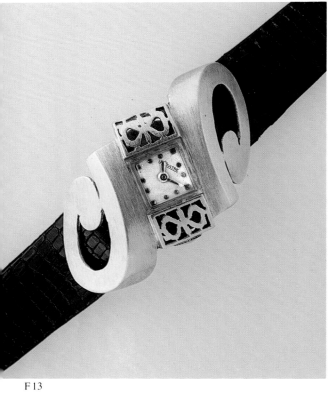

F 13

F 14

F11 Gruen, USA/Switzerland
Circa 1926. Platinum hinged case set with diamonds. Stem-wind. Oval anchor movement, extra quality. 18 jewels, 6 bearings adjustable. Breguet hairspring. Bimetallic balance. Flexible attachments.
(Joseph) $720-810

F12 LeCoultre
Circa 1925. 935 hinged silver case with black, green and blue enamel. Stem-wind. Formed anchor movement. 15 jewels. Flat hairspring. Bimetallic balance. The band appears to be a "ribbon band."
(Joseph) $720-810

F13 LeCoultre
Circa 1950. Matte 15-karat yellow-gold designer case. Stem-wind. Caliber 490 BW. 17 jewels. Breguet hairspring. Bimetallic balance.
(Joseph) $720-900

F14 LeCoultre
Circa 1950. 14-karat yellow-gold case with lid over dial containing picture frame. LeCoultre 490 BW caliber, ornamental formed movement. 17 jewels. Breguet hairspring. Bimetallic balance. Rare design.
(Joseph) $810-990

F15 Huber/Movado
Stainless steel case, very arched. Stem-wind. 9 by 13-ligne formed movement. 15 jewels. 4 chatons. Breguet hairspring. Bimetallic balance. Arched front plate.
(Privately owned) $1,350-1,620

F16 Durbin with spring lid
1950. Gold-filled case. Stem-wind. Swiss anchor movement. 17 jewels. Flat hairspring. Monometallic screw balance.
(Joseph) $270-470

F17 Anonymous Masonic Watch
Eighties. Gilded metal case. 17 jewels. Flat hairspring. Glucydur balance. Incabloc shock resistance.
(Henrys) $450-540

F15 A

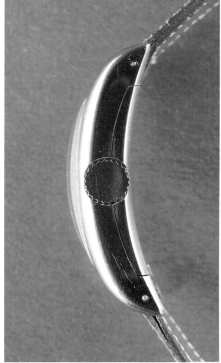

F15 B

F16

F17

F18

F19

F18 Mickey Mouse Watch
(Disneyland)
1980. Chromed metal case. Rosskop
movement, Bettlach caliber.
(Privately owned) $90-135

F19 Anonymous
Forties. Chromed nickel case. Rosskop
movement. Woody Woodpecker dia
design.
(Privately owned) $180-270

F20 Six Puff-Swatches
1988   complete $4,500-5,400

F20

Catalog Illustrations

Early Wristwatches

The watch moved onto the wrist in the 16th century. Yet the examples produced until about 1850 are actually just forerunners. Early wristwatches were made in the period up to about 1920. In many cases, they could not deny their descent, in terms of form, from the pocket watch. But the watch manufacturers were already beginning to experiment with the wristwatch at that time. The form of the dial and the case were no longer taboo. It was in fact necessary if they wanted to help this new type of watch find acceptance, especially among conservative men. Among collectors, these early wristwatches have thus far awakened only limited interest. The reason is that they are less suited for daily use than to preservation in a showcase. This means that early wristwatches can still be bought for relatively reasonable prices.

2

3

4

5

6

7

1 Pavel Buhré
Circa 1912. Hinged nickel case. Enameled dial. Stem-wind. 15 jewels. Flat hairspring. Bimetallic balance.
(Henrys) $675-1,080

2 Vacheron & Constantin for DENT Circa 1910 Silver, half-hunting case. Special feature: pin-set; the time is set by pushing in the button at 2:00 and turning the crown. Stem wind. Swiss cylinder movement. 15 jewels. Flat hairspring. Bimetallic balance.
(Privately owned) $1,260-1,620

3. Tavannes
Circa 1915. 925 silver, 2 rear couvettes with a hunting case which opens by pushing the button by the 6. Stem-wind. 15 jewels. 3 chatons. Flat hairspring. Bimetallic balance. Enameled dial, hour hand later.
(Joseph) $270-450

4 IWC
Circa 1915. 18-karat gold, signed B & C, no. 670742. Movement screwed into case. 2/3-plate movement, no. 622128. 15 jewels, screwed chatons. Breguet hairspring. Bimetallic balance. Enameled dial.
(Henrys) $720-1,080

5 Zenith for U.S. Army Signal Corps
Circa 1918. Silver hinged case. Stem-wind. Gilded anchor movement. 15 jewels. Breguet hairspring. Bimetallic balance. Fine regulation via eccentric, red XII, red 24-hour scale.
(Henrys) $450-630

6 Anonymous, Swiss
Circa 1918. 935 silver hinged case. Stem-wind. Nickel movement. 15 jewels. Flat hairspring. Monometallic screw balance. Black enameled dial.
(Henrys) $270-450

7 Anonymous, Swiss
Circa 1912. Silver, English case. Movement screwed into case. Stem-wind. Swiss raw movement, nickel-plated. 15 jewels. Breguet hairspring. Bimetallic balance. Hands later. Enameled dial, red XII.
(Henrys) $225-270

8 Ingersoll
1917. Nickel. Pin lever (American low-priced watch no. 45801468). No jewels. Monometallic balance. Special feature: Winding stem by the 12. Glued-on certificate of origin.
(Privately owned) $90-180

9 IWC
Circa 1917. 18-karat gold. Screwed case, no. 671788. 11.75 lignes, IWC 64 caliber. 17 jewels, some in chatons. Breguet hairspring. Bimetallic balance. Special feature: To screw the movement out, the crown must be pulled.
(Privately owned) $810-1,260

10 Rolex
Circa 1915. Silver hunting case, no. 773207. Stem-wind. Pearlized German silver movement. 15 jewels. Flat hairspring. Bimetallic balance. Button by the 6 opens the case.
(Privately owned) $1,260-1,620

11 Anonymous, Swiss
Circa 1920. Nickel. Central second. Stem-wind. Cylinder escapement. 4 jewels. Flat hairspring. Monometallic balance. Nurse's watch.
(Privately owned) $135-180

12 Patek Philippe
1925. Gold, two-hinge lid. Enameled dial with 12-and 24-hour scales. Stem-wind, no 805277, 9 lignes, 3rd quality. Ebauche by LeCoultre. 15 jewels. Flat hairspring. Bimetallic balance.
(Privately owned) $6.300-8,100

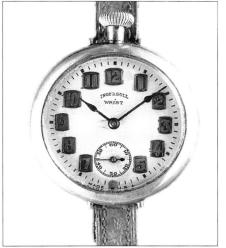

8

9

10 A

10 B

11

12

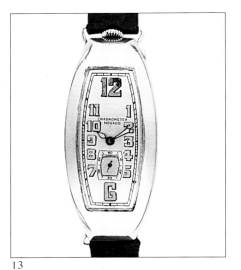

13

14

15

16

17

18

13 Movado Chronometer
Circa 1920. Hinged silver case. Poly-plan (angled plate). Stem-wind. 15 jewels. Breguet hairspring. Bimetallic balance. Very arched case form. Winding stem by the 12.
(Privately owned) $2,250-2,700

14 Anonymous, Swiss
Late twenties. Hinged silver case. Stem-wind. Swiss cylinder movement. 9 jewels. Flat hairspring. Monometallic balance. Round 12-ligne movement in overlong rectangular case. Hands later. Luminous numerals.
(Hein) $810-900

15 IWC for Mappin & Webb
Circa 1917. 925 silver hinged case. Stem-wind. Caliber 64. 15 jewels. Breguet hairspring. Bimetallic balance. Hand-setting button.
(Joseph) $1,620-2,250

16 Anonymous
Circa 1920. Tula silver. Carrée Cambrée form (pillow-shaped). 15 jewels. Flat hairspring. Bimetallic balance. Hand-setting button by the 4.
(Henrys) $180-270

17 Omega
Circa 1925. Hinged silver case. Stem-wind. Gilt movement. 15 jewels. Breguet hairspring. Bimetallic balance.
(Breitsprecher) $360-540

18 Omega
Circa 1920. Hinged silver case. Stem-wind. Movement no. 5055492. 15 jewels. Breguet hairspring. Bimetallic balance. Typical watch of the early twenties.
(Privately owned) $720-1,080

19

20

21

22

23

19 Various Swiss men's wristwatches
Early twenties. Silver. Stem-wind. Swiss movements. Enameled dials.
(Henrys) $270-540

20 Patek Philippe
Twenties. 18-karat yellow gold. Stem-wind. 12-ligne caliber, third quality. 15 jewels. Flat hairspring. Bimetallic balance. Dial with typical decoration of the time.
(Privately owned) $3,600-5,400

21 Longines
Twenties. 18-karat yellow gold. Carrée Cambrée form. Caliber 13.3. 15 jewels. Breguet hairspring. Bimetallic balance. Enameled dial.
(Joseph) $360-540

22 Ulysse Nardin
Circa 1925. Gold pillow-shaped case. Stem-wind. 15 jewels. Bimetallic balance. Crown later.
(Henrys) $540-720

23 Eberhard
Circa 1920. Silver pillow-shaped case. Stem-wind. Gilt movement. 15 jewels. Breguet hairspring. Bimetallic balance. Enameled dial.
(Henrys) $180-315

24

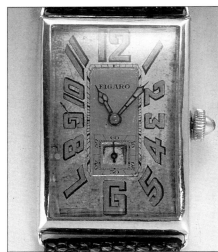

25

26

27

28

29

24 Anonymous

Twenties. Silver case, screwed on the sides. Stem-wind. Round anchor movement. 15 jewels. Flat hairspring. Screw balance. Restored dial.
(Privately owned) $1,080-1,260

25 Figaro, Swiss

Circa 1930. 14-karat yellow gold hanged case. Stem-wind. 15 jewels. Flat hairspring. Bimetallic balance. Luminous numerals and hands.
(Breitsprecher) $720-900

26 Rolex

Late twenties. Silver tonneau-shaped hinged case, no. 819819. Stem-wind. Round Rolex "Prima" movement. Bimetallic balance.
(Henrys) $1,350-1,620

27 Agassiz for Gübelin

Late twenties. 18-karat yellow gold. Typical fine flexible band. Stem-wind. 6 adjustments. 18 jewels. Breguet hairspring. Bimetallic balance.
(Henrys) $1,620-2,160

28 Rolex

Late twenties. 925 silver Oyster case. First waterproof watch. Stem-wind. Oyster "Prima" quality, adjustable to 6 positions. 15 jewels. Flat hairspring. Bimetallic balance. Restored dial.
(Henrys) $1,620-2,160

29 IWC

Circa 1930. Hinged 14-karat yellow-gold pillow-shaped case. Stem-wind. Caliber 76, 10.33 lignes. 16 jewels, some in chatons. Breguet hairspring. Bimetallic balance.
(Henrys) $1,260-1,440

Ladies' Wristwatches

Although the ladies helped the overall success of the wristwatch, the ladies' watch - with few exceptions - has never attained the status of a collector's item. Among other reasons, this may be so because the ladies' watch was fully developed in terms of form, but in technical terms never had more than a small number of variations. In addition, the area of wristwatch collecting has been a man's domain to this day, and the male collectors generally give preference to watches that they themselves can wear. Therefore one can buy ladies' watches of the finest quality at prices well below those of comparable men's models.

31

32

33

34

35

30 Vacheron & Constantin

Circa 1935. Hinged platinum case with diamonds and sapphires. Stem-wind. Formed anchor movement. 18 jewels, adjustable in five positions. Breguet hairspring. Bimetallic balance. Ribbon band with platinum clasp.
(Joseph)　$16,200-18,000

31 "Election," Swiss, for the British market

Circa 1927. Hinged 9-karat gold case. White and blue enameled bezel. Stem-wind. Swiss anchor movement. 15 jewels. Flat hairspring. Screw balance. Metal dial with red 12.
(Breitsprecher)　$270-360

32 Anonymous, Swiss, for the British market

Circa 1912. Hinged sterling silver case. Stem-wind. Gilt swiss cylinder movement. 10 jewels. Flat hairspring. Monometallic screw balance. Special features: Hand-setting via crown and button by the 4, enameled dial with red 12.(Breitsprecher) $225-270

33 Anonymous, Swiss

Circa 1912. Yellow gold with enameled decorative panel. Stem-wind. 9-ligne caliber, anchor movement, second-quality ebauche by LeCoultre. 18 jewels. Flat hairspring. Bimetallic balance. Hand-setting via crown and button by the 2. Enameled dial.
(Sothebys) $1,620-1,980

34 Anonymous, Swiss, for Brooks & Son, England

Circa 1890. Rose gold. Pocket watch set on decorative band to be worn as a wristwatch. Swiss cylinder movement. 15 jewels. Flat hairspring. Bimetallic balance. Enameled dial.
(Joseph)　$810-1,080

35 Anonymous, Swiss

Early twenties. Hinged silver case. Stem-wind. Nickel-plated movement. 15 jewels. Flat hairspring. Monometallic screw balance. $900-1,080

36 C. H. Meylan
Circa 1920. Octagonal plate, hinged case. Silver dial with blue numerals. Stem-wind. 8-ligne lapidary anchor movement. 18 jewels, 5 positions adjustable. Breguet hairspring. Screw balance.
(Joseph) $900-1,080

37 Jaeger LeCoultre
Circa 1955. 18-karat rose gold. Back-wind caliber. Stem-wind. 17 jewels.
(Privately owned) $540-720

38 Blancpain
Sixties. 18-karat gold. Stem-wind. Backwind caliber. 17 jewels. Flat hairspring. Monometallic screw balance.
(Privately owned) $450-720

39 Paul Ditisheim
Circa 1940. 18-karat rose gold. Red colored stones and diamonds. Stem-wind. Formed anchor movement. 17 jewels. Flat hairspring. Monometallic balance.
(Joseph) $540-720

40 Lucien Picard
Circa 1955. 14-karat yellow-gold case with spring lid (set with pearls). Backwind caliber. 17 jewels, some in gold chatons. Breguet hairspring. Bimetallic balance. Shock resistance.
(Joseph) $720-900

41 Patek Philippe
1937. 18-karat yellow and red gold. No. 497. Stem-wind. 9-ligne caliber, second quality. 18 jewels. Flat hairspring. Bimetallic balance.
(Privately owned) $3,600-5,400

36

37

38

39

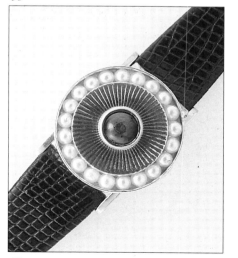

40

41

42

43

44

45

46   47

42 LeCoultre
Circa 1940. Stainless steel. Reverso case. Stem-wind. Gilt formed movement. 15 jewels. Flat hairspring. Monometallic screw balance.
(Joseph) $1,800-1,980

43 Gruen
Thirties Steel "Doctor's Watch" in ladies size. Stem-wind. Formed movement. 17 jewels. Flat hairspring. Bimetallic balance.
(Privately owned) $540-720

44 Jaeger
Circa 1935. Hinged stainless steel case. Stem-wind, back crown for winding and hand-setting. Duoplan caliber 9 BF. 15 jewels, 2 positions adjustable. Breguet hairspring. Bimetallic balance.
(Joseph) $360-540

45 Jaeger LeCoultre Reverso
Circa 1938. Steel and 14-karat gold turning (Reverso) case. Stem-wind. Caliber 26, octagonal formed movement. 15 jewels. Flat hairspring. Monometallic screw balance. Ladies' Reverso watches are rare.
(Henrys) $1,800-1,980

46 Ato-Rolls Automatic
Circa 1930. 18-karat yellow gold hinged case. Inside crown for hand-setting. Winding by moving the movement longitudinally over balls in lateral rails. Patent by Léon Hatot, 1930. Built by Blancpain. 5.5 lignes. 17 jewels. Flat hairspring. Bimetallic balance. Early automatic watch.
(Christies) $720-900

47 Mimo (Girard Perregaux)
Circa 1930. 14-karat white-gold hinged case. Stem-wind. Formed anchor movement. 15 jewels. 4 positions adjustable. Breguet hairspring. Bimetallic balance. Ribbon band.
(Joseph) $270-450

48 Tiffany, New York, with Swiss movement
Circa 1930. Platinum and white gold. 4-karat old-cut diamonds. Stem-wind. Oval 9-ligne formed movement. 17 jewels. Flat hairspring. Compensated balance.
(Privately owned) $3,150-4,050

49 Patek Philippe for T. & D. Dickinson, USA
Late twenties. Platinum with diamonds. Cord band. 14-karat yellow gold. Nickel-plated formed movement, no. 200129. 6 adjustments. Stem-wind. 18 jewels. Compensated balance. Platinum crown.
(Henrys) $2,520-3,420

50 Bulova
Circa 1925. 14-karat gold case, upper part enameled red and blue. Stem-wind. Formed anchor movement. Caliber 3 AN. Swiss movement, U.S. case. 7 jewels. Flat hairspring. Screw balance. (Joseph) $360-450

51 Rolex
Circa 1927. 18-karat white gold. 2 x 6 rubies. Stem-wind. Oval formed movement. Rolex Extra Prima. 15 jewels. Flat hairspring. Bimetallic balance. Typical art deco watch.
(Henrys) $720-900

52 Anonymous, Swiss
Circa 1915. 18-karat yellow gold. Bezel with diamonds and sapphires. Rear lid enameled red. Stem-wind. Bridge movement with cylinder escapement. Flat hairspring. Monometallic balance. Enameled dial with blue 24-hour scale.
(Joseph) $180-270

53 Anonymous
Circa 1900. Gold-plated. Lady's pendulum watch with plated link band, to be worn as wristwatch. 9 lignes. Cylinder movement. 7 jewels. Flat hairspring. Enameled dial.
(Privately owned) $180-270

48

49

50

51

52

53

54

Formed Wristwatches

Formed wristwatches arose from the need to free the wristwatch from its formal ties to the design of the pocket watch. Ranked among formed wristwatches are all models that depart from the classic round style, such as those with pillow-shaped, diamond-shaped or barrel-shaped cases. The models in rectangular and square form, though, have become most widespread. Rectangular wristwatches reached their zenith in the thirties, when an unequaled variety of case and movement types came into being. The fifties were the decade of the square wristwatch.

Among collectors, the rectangular wristwatch has much greater interest than the square one. For that reason, their prices - assuming the same level of quality - are also higher as a rule. Beyond that, the rarity, extravagance and/or the brand name determine the market price.

54 Elgin
1928. 18-karat white gold. Blue enameled ring, flexible attachments. Stemwind. 15 jewels, 3 screwed chatons. Breguet hairspring. Bimetallic compensated balance.
(Privately owned) $1,080-1,350

55 Rolex
Twenties. 9-karat tonneau form. Stemwind. Round anchor movement. 15 jewels. Flat hairspring. Bimetallic balance. Restored dial.
(Privately owned) $1,350-1,620

56 A. LeCoultre
Twenties. 14-karat yellow gold hinged case. Stem-wind. 15 jewels. Flat hairspring. Bimetallic balance.
(Joseph) $1,080-1,620

57 Anonymous
1920. Screwed chrome-plated case. So-called hospital witch. Central second. Caliber 970. 15 jewels. Monometallic balance.
(Henrys) $360-450

58 Mido, Watches in car radiator form (Bugatti, etc.)
18-karat gold. Stem-wind. 8.75-ligne caliber. 15 jewels. Flat hairspring.
(Crott) $4,500-6,750

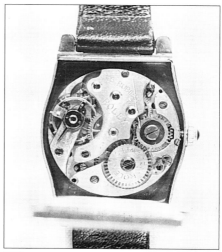

55 A

55 B

56

57

58 A

58 B

59

60

61

62

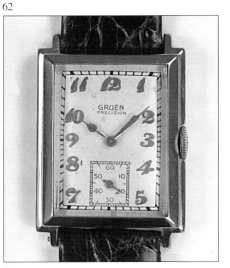

63

64

59 Hamilton
Circa 1937. 9-karat yellow gold-filled case. Black dial. Stem-wind. Caliber 980. 17 jewels. Breguet hairspring. Bimetallic balance. Duo-Dial model.
(Breitsprecher) $810-1,080

60 Eterna
1930. Stainless steel. Stem-wind. 8.75 lignes Caliber 675. 15 jewels. Flat hairspring.
(Privately owned) $270-540

61 Rolex Chronometer
Circa 1930. Rectangular stainless steel case. Stem-wind. Nickel-plated formed movement. Two adjustments, 17 jewels. Breguet hairspring. Monometallic screw balance.
(Henrys) $1,260-1,800

62 Bulova
Circa 1939. 10-karat gold-filled case. Formed anchor movement. Stem-wind. Caliber 7 AP. Breguet hairspring. Monometallic screw balance.
(Privately owned) $315-405

63 Auréole
1930. Chrome-plated nickel. Laterally stepped case. Stem-wind. Caliber 7.5 by 11 lignes. Flat hairspring. Monometallic balance.
(Privately owned) $225-315

64 Gruen
Circa 1935. 14-karat yellow gold case with ornamented sides. Stem-wind. Formed "Precision Extra" movement, 8.75 by 11 lignes. 17 jewels. Breguet hairspring. Bimetallic balance.
(Privately owned) $405-450

65 Patek Philippe
1933. 18-karat yellow gold "motorist's watch." Stem-wind. Rectangular formed work, 8 lignes. 18 jewels. Ebauche by LeCoultre. Flat hairspring. Bimetallic balance.
(Patek) $6,300-8,820

66 Niton
Circa 1930. 18-karat yellow gold, stepped case. Special features: Hour indication in aperture, springing, minutes on disc, small second. Stem-wind. Breguet hairspring.
(Crott) $8,100-10,800

67 Doxa
1932. Hinged silver case. Stem-wind. Formed movement. 15 jewels. Flat hairspring. Bimetallic balance.
(Breitsprecher) $270-315

68 Optima
1934. 14-karat yellow gold hinged case. Stem-wind. 15 jewels. Flat hairspring. Bimetallic balance.
(Breitsprecher) $270-360

69 Patek Philippe
1933. 18-karat yellow gold. Stem-wind. No. 821550, 8-ligne caliber, second quality. Raw movement by LeCoultre. 23 jewels. Breguet hairspring. Bimetallic balance.
(Patek) $5,400-7,200

70 Vacheron & Constantin
Thirties/forties. 18-karat yellow gold. Formed movement. Breguet hairspring. Bimetallic balance.
(Privately owned) $3,150-4,050

65

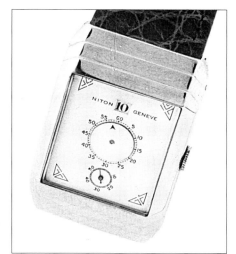

66

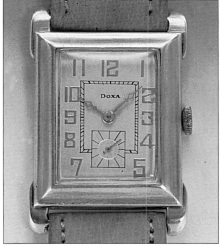

67

68

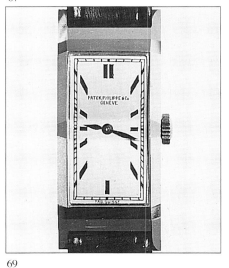

69

70

71

72

73

74

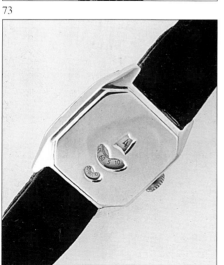

75

76

71 Audax
Circa 1935. 9-karat gold English hinged case. Stem-wind. Gilt formed movement. 15 jewels. Monometallic screw balance.
(Privately owned) $315-405

72 Gruen Curvex
Circa 1938. Gold-plated, steel base. Swiss formed movement. Caliber 300. 15 jewels. Breguet hairspring. Monometallic screw balance.
(Privately owned) $720-1,080

73 Anonymous
Circa 1935. Hinged 9-karat gold (English) case. Special features: Digital indication, springing hour, sliding minute and second. Stem-wind. Tonneau-shaped raw anchor movement by **FHF**. 16 jewels. Flat hairspring. Monometallic screw balance.
(Henrys) $1,080-1,350

74 Gruen
Circa 1936. Stainless steel, springing hour in window. Stem-wind. Large Swiss formed anchor movement, Caliber 877 S. 17 jewels. Breguet hairspring. Screw balance. Movement identical to Rolex "Prince."
(Henrys) $2,250-3,150

75 Anonymous
Circa 1932. White gold. Springing hour, sliding minute and second. Stem-wind. Swiss formed movement. 15 jewels. Flat hairspring. Monometallic screw balance.
(Joseph) $1,080-1,350

76 Paul Ditisheim
Circa 1938. Platinum. Special feature: Diamond numerals set in white gold. Tonneau-shaped formed movement. 17 jewels. Breguet hairspring. Monometallic screw balance.
(Henrys) $2,700-3,150

77 A. Lange u. Söhne, Glashütte
Thirties. Stainless steel. V 2 A. Stem-
wind. Formed anchor movement by
Altus. Caliber 10, 8.75 by 12 lignes. 16
jewels. Flat hairspring. Compensated
balance. (Joseph) $2,700-3,600

78 Doxa
Circa 1935. Stainless steel. Arched
hinged case. Stem-wind. 17 jewels.
Flat hairspring. Monometallic screw
balance. (Joseph) $180-360

79 Uhrenfabrik Glashütte
Circa 1936. 14-karat yellow gold.
Stem-wind. Gilt formed movement,
9 by 13 lignes, Urofa Caliber 58. 15
jewels. Breguet hairspring. Screw
balance.
(Joseph) $720-900

80 Elgin
Circa 1935. 10-karat gold-filled case.
Doctor's Watch, #5509. Stem-wind.
Formed movement. 17 jewels. Flat
hairspring.
(Joseph) $630-675

81 Longines
Circa 1938. Chrome-plated brass.
Stem-wind. 15 jewels. Breguet hair-
spring. Bimetallic balance.
(Joseph) $1,350-1,800

82 Gruen Doctor's Watch
Circa 1935. White-gold-filled case.
Divided dial. Stem-wind. Caliber 877
S. 15 jewels. Breguet hairspring. Bime-
tallic balance.
(Henrys) $450-720

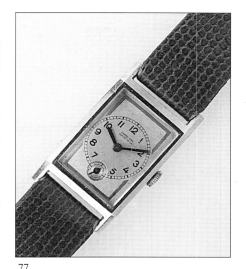

77

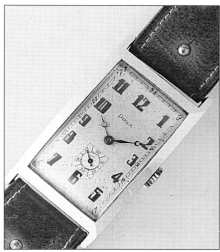

78

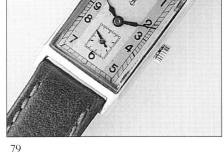

79

80

81

82

83

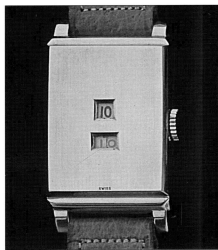

84

85

86

87

88

83 IWC
Circa 1935. Stainless steel case. Stem-wind. Lapidary formed anchor movement. Caliber 87.17 jewels. Breguet hairspring. Monometallic screw balance.
(Joseph) $1,620-2,250

84 Movado
Thirties. 14-karat yellow gold. Disc for hour indication, 2 discs for minute indication. Stem-wind. 15 jewels. Breguet hairspring. Bimetallic balance. Special feature: Digital indication, very rare.
(Privately owned) $2,250-3,150

85 Longines
Circa 1935. Platinum. Black dial with diamond numerals set in white gold. Stem-wind. Caliber 9 lignes. 17 jewels. Flat hairspring. Monometallic screw balance.
(Joseph) $1,080-2,700

86 Rolex Prince Chronometer, "Brancard" type
Stem-wind. Extra Prima caliber. 15 jewels. Breguet hairspring. Monometallic screw balance. Special feature: Stripes white and yellow-gold case.
(A. Bauer) $8,100-10,800

87 Waltham
Thirties. 14-karat yellow gold. Stem-wind.
(Privately owned) $270-405

88 Rolex Prince for the Eaton firm's 1/4 Century Club
Thirties. 14-karat yellow gold. Stem-wind. Caliber 300. 15 jewels. Breguet hairspring. Super-balance balance.
(Privately owned) $5,400-6,300

89 A

89 B

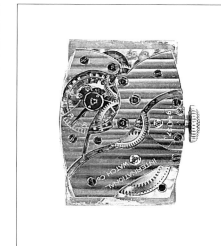

89 C

89 IWC
Forties. 18-karat yellow gold. Lovely case engraved on sides. Stem-wind. Movement no. 944157, 8.75 by 11 lignes. Formed movement. Caliber 87. 17 jewels. Breguet hairspring. Bimetallic balance.
(Privately owned) $1,980-2,250

90 Movado
1940. 14-karat yellow gold. Flexible attachments. Round stem-wind movement. 17 jewels. Flat hairspring. Monometallic screw balance.
(Voithenberg) $720-1,080

91 Helvetia
1940. Stainless steel. Waterproof. Stem-wind. Movement no. 120138. 15 jewels. 3 adjustments. Flat hairspring. Bimetallic balance. Shock resistance. Luminous numerals and hands.
(Privately owned) $270-360

92 Movado
1940. 14-karat yellow gold. Round stem-wind movement. Caliber 150 M. 17 jewels. Flat hairspring. Bimetallic balance. Special feature: unusual attachments.
(A. Bauer) $720-1,080

90

91

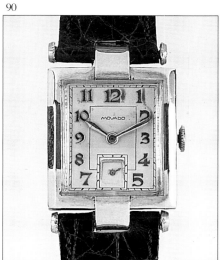

92 A

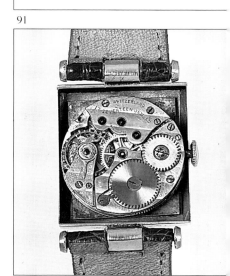

92 B

93

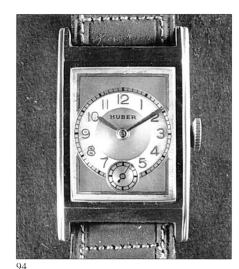

94

95

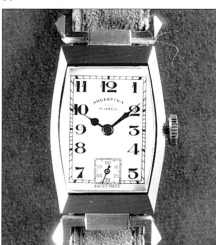

96

97

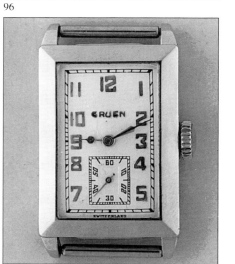

98

93 Helvetia
1940. Stainless steel. Stem-wind. Formed movement. 15 jewels. Flat hairspring. Monometallic screw balance. Shock resistance. Covered band attachments.
(Privately owned) $180-270

94 Huber, Munich
Forties. Steel case. Stem-wind. Caliber 717 by Eta. Formed movement, 8.75 by 12 lignes. 17 jewels. Breguet hairspring. Monometallic balance. Screw balance.
(Privately owned) $270-315

95 Huber, Munich
1940. Stainless steel. Stem-wind. Caliber 20/26 T by Moeris, Switzerland. 15 jewels. Flat hairspring. Monometallic screw balance. Shock resistance.
(Privately owned) $270-315

96 Argentina
Forties. Steel case. Stem-wind. Formed movement, 7.75 by 11 lignes. 15 jewels. Flat hairspring. Monometallic screw balance. Flexible attachments.
(Privately owned) $180-225

97 Jaeger-LeCoultre
1940. Waterproof steel case. Stem-wind. Formed movement, 7.75 by 11 lignes. 15 jewels. Flat hairspring. Beryllium balance.
(Privately owned) $450-900

98 Gruen
1940. Steel case. Stem-wind. Formed movement. Gruen Guild 157, Swiss. 15 jewels. 4 adjustments. Breguet hairspring. Bimetallic balance.
(Privately owned) $180-225

99 Bulova
Circa 1942. 10-karat gold-filed case.
Stem-wind. Formed anchor movement
6 AE. 21 jewels. Breguet hairspring.
Monometallic screw balance.
(Henrys) $225-360

100 Elgin
Circa 1940. 14-karat red gold. White
gold numerals, art deco style. Stem-
wind. Bridge movement. 15 jewels,
some in screwed chatons. Geneva
stripes. (Henrys) $450-540

101 Gruen Curvex Precision
Circa 1948. 14-karat gold. Stem-wind.
Caliber 370. 17 jewels. Breguet hair-
spring. Monometallic screw balance.
Partly covered attachments.
(Henrys) $405-495

102 LeCoultre
Circa 1944. 14-karat yellow gold.
Central band attachments. Stem-wind.
Caliber 438/4 CW, octagonal formed
movement. 17 jewels. Flat hairspring.
Glucydur balance.
(Privately owned) $1,350-1,440

103 Girard Peregaux
Circa 1942. 14-karat yellow gold.
Stem-wind. Formed movement. 17
jewels, some in chatons. Flat hairspring. Glucydur balance. Special feature: lateral case reinforcement later.
(Henrys) $730-720

104 Patek Philippe
Circa 1941. 950 platinum case. Formed
anchor movement, no. 831383,
9-ligne-90 caliber. 18 jewels. Flat
hairspring. Glucydur balance. Restored dial.
(Henrys) $4,500-9,000

99

100

101

102

103

104

105

106

107 A

107 B

108

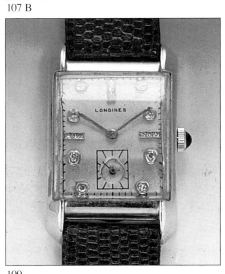

109

105 LeCoultre
Circa 1944. 14-karat white gold. Covered ornamental attachments. Diamonds mark the hours. Stem-wind. Octagonal formed movement, Caliber 438/4 CW. 15 jewels. Flat hairspring. Glucydur balance.
(Henrys) $450-720

106 LeCoultre
Circa 1948. 18-karat yellow gold. Stem-wind. Gilt lapidary formed movement. 17 jewels. Flat hairspring. Monometallic screw balance.
(Joseph) $1,080-1,260

107 Movado
1940. 14-karat yellow gold. Stem-wind. Caliber 510, 8.75 by 12-ligne formed movement. 17 jewels. Flat hairspring. Glucydur balance.
(Voithenberg) $900-1,170

108 Vacheron & Constantin
1940. 18-karat yellow gold. Stem-wind. LeCoultre caliber. 18 jewels. Breguet hairspring. Screw balance.
(Voithenberg) $4,050-5,400

109 Longines
Circa 1940. 14-karat yellow gold. Diamonds mark hours. Stem-wind. Caliber 22 lignes. 17 jewels. Breguet hairspring. Bimetallic balance.
(Breitsprecher) $540-675

110 Vacheron & Constantin
Early forties. 18-karat yellow gold.
Movement no. 471597. Stem-wind.
Caliber V 458. 17 jewels. Breguet hair-
spring. Monometallic screw balance.
(Privately owned) $1,620-2,160

111 Longines
Circa 1948. 14-karat yellow gold. Tab-
let-shaped glass. Stem-wind. Caliber
25.17 (9LT). 17 jewels. Flat hairspring.
Glucydur hairspring.
(Henrys) $900-1,080

112 Doxa
Circa 1947. Stainless steel case. Stem-
wind. 17 jewels. Flat hairspring. Monometallic screw balance.
(Joseph) $270-360

113 Longines
Forties. 14-karat yellow gold. Unusual
attachments. Stem-wind. Caliber 22
lignes. 17 jewels. Flat hairspring. Glucydur balance.
(Breitsprecher) $900-1,080

110 A

110 B

111

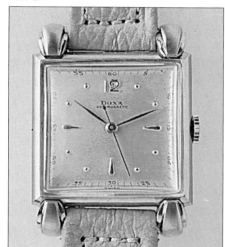

112

113

114

115

116

117

118

119

114 LeCoultre "Grashopper"
1952. 10-karat gold-filled case. Stem-wind. Lapidary formed anchor movement. Caliber 438/4 CW. 17 jewels. Flat hairspring. Glucydur balance.
(Joseph) $1,080-1,350

115 Universal
Circa 1954. 18-karat rose gold. Stem-wind. Caliber 264. 15 jewels. Flat hairspring. Bimetallic balance.
(Breitsprecher) $720-900

116 Longines "Advocate"
1952. 14-karat yellow gold. Set diamonds mark hours on dial. Stem-wind. Formed anchor movement. Caliber 9 LT. 17 jewels. Flat hairspring. Glucydur balance.
(Joseph) $720-810

117 Cartier "Curvex Banana"
Circa 1960. 18-karat yellow gold. Stem-wind. Rhodinized anchor movement by Bueche Girod, Geneva. 17 jewels, 5 adjusted positions. Geneva stripes. Flat hairspring. Glucydur balance. Shock resistance.
(Henrys) $3,600-4,500

118 Universal
Circa 1960. 18-karat yellow gold. Stem-wind. Caliber 500. 17 jewels. Self-compensating flat hairspring. Monometallic screw balance. Shock resistance. (Joseph) $450-630

119 Corum "Buckingham"
1978. 18-karat yellow gold. Covered attachments. Stem-wind. No. 5789/31. Basic movement by Rayvill, Calibre 4200. 21 jewels. Flat hairspring. Glucydur balance.
(Henrys) $1,350-1,620

120

Hand-wound Wristwatches

Although classic wristwatches with manual winding look very similar externally, their interiors can show great differences. Behind the facade of a rather unknown name, a seemingly bourgeois dial, and an unadorned case there can be hidden technical features. Discovering them requires technical knowledge and a trained eye. Thus one has the chance of obtaining an outstanding specimen of wristwatch history at a comparatively favorable price.

121

122

123

124

125

126

120 Rolex Precision
1943. 18-karat yellow gold. No. 3750.
17 jewels. Central second. Breguet
hairspring. Superbalance.
(Henrys) $1,800-2,050

121 Omega
Circa 1933. Stainless steel case. Stem-
wind. Caliber 26.5. 15 jewels. Breguet
hairspring. Bimetallic balance.
(Henrys) $450-720

122 Cyma de Luxe
Circa 1938. Pillow-shaped steel case.
No. 234. Stem-wind. 15 jewels. Flat
hairspring. Monometallic screw balance. (Henrys) $225-270

123 Movado Chronoplan
1937. Stainless steel. Two turning outside bezels to count hours and minutes.
Stem-wind. 15 jewels. 4 adjustments.
Breguet hairspring. Bimetallic compensated balance.
(Privately owned) $540-720

124 A.Lange u. Söhne,Glashütte
1930. 14-karat gold. Stem-wind. No
81475. 3/4 platinum movement. Gold
anchor wheel. Breguet hairspring. Bimetallic balance with gold screws.
(Crott) $2,250-3,150

125 Rolex
Late thirties. Pillow-shaped 9-karat
gold case. Stem-wind. 15 jewels.
Breguet hairspring. Bimetallic balance.
Restored dial.
(Privately owned) $1,050-1,800

126 Universal
Late thirties. Pillow-shaped 14-karat
gold case. Stem-wind. 17 jewels. Flat
hairspring. Restored dial.
(Privately owned) $1,080-1,450

127 Longines
Early forties. 18-karat red gold case.
Stem-wind. 16 jewels. Central second.
Flat hairspring. Bimetallic balance.
(Breitsprecher) $540-630

128 Rolex
Circa 1943. Square steel case. No.
4031. 17 jewels. Indirect central second. Superbalance.
(Henrys) $1,800-2,700

129 Patek Philippe "Calatrava"
Forties. 18-karat yellow gold. Stem-wind. Caliber 12-120. 18 jewels. Temperature and 5 position adjustments. Breguet hairspring. Glucydur balance.
(Joseph) $5,400-6,300 * With Breguet-Zuhle ca. 10,000.

130 Ulysse Nardin
Forties. Stainless steel. Stem-wind. 18 jewels. Breguet hairspring. Glucydur balance.
(Privately owned) $720-900

131 Patek Philippe
Forties. 18-karat yellow gold. No. 1528. Stem-wind. 12-ligne 120 caliber. 18 jewels. Breguet hairspring. Glucydur balance.
(Privately owned) $3,600-4,500

132 Vacheron & Constantin
Forties. 18-karat gold. Stem-wind. 17 jewels. Crown by the XII.
(Mercier) $3,600-4,500

127

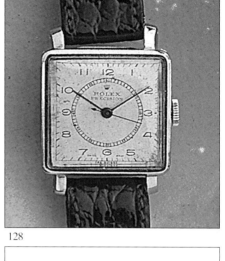

128

129

130

131

132

133

134

135

136

137 A

137 B

133 IWC

Forties. 18-karat yellow gold. Stem-wind. 12-ligne. Caliber 83. 16 jewels. Breguet hairspring. Bimetallic balance. Incabloc shock resistance.
(Breitsprecher) $1,368-1,620

134 Omega

Forties. Stainless steel. Stem-wind. Caliber 30 T 2. 16 jewels. Breguet hairspring. Bimetallic balance. Central second.
(Breitsprecher) $305-405

135 Patek Philippe

Forties. 18-karat yellow gold. No. 1491. Arched band attachments. Stem-wind. 12-ligne 120 caliber. 18 jewels. Breguet hairspring. Glucydur balance.
(Breitsprecher) $5,400-7,200

136 Moeris

Forties. Steel case. Rotating bezel. Stem-wind. Moeris caliber. 17 jewels. Flat hairspring. Glucydur balance.
(Privately owned) $135-180

137 Zenith

1940. 18-karat gold. Stem-wind for US market. 11.25 lignes. 15 jewels. Breguet hairspring. Bimetallic balance. Demascened movement. Restored dial.
(Privately owned) $540-720

138 Omega
Circa 1940. Stainless steel. Waterproof.
Stem-wind. 17 jewels. Flat hairspring.
Compensated balance.
(Breitsprecher) $450-540

139 Longines
Circa 1945. 14-karat white gold. Stem-
wind. Caliber 22 lignes. Diamonds
mark hours. Breguet hairspring. Monometallic screw balance.
(Henrys) $900-1,080

140 IWC Mark XI
As of 1948. Stainless steel. 12-ligne
Caliber 89. 17 jewels. Breguet hair-
spring. Indirect central second. Glu-
cydur balance, stopped by the crown.
Incabloc shock resistance.
(IWC) $3,150-3,600

141 Omega
Circa 1949. Screwed stainless steel
case. Stem-wind. Caliber 266. 17
jewels. Breguet hairspring. Self-compensating balance. Incabloc shock
resistance. (Breitsprecher) $315-450

**142 Tavannes-Cyma military
watch.** Late forties. Stainless steel.
Stem-wind. 15 jewels. Breguet hairspring. Glucydur balance.
(Privately owned) $405-585

138

139

140

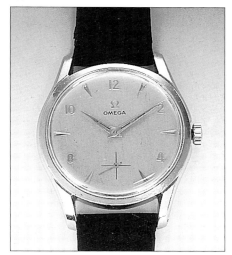

141

142 A

142 B

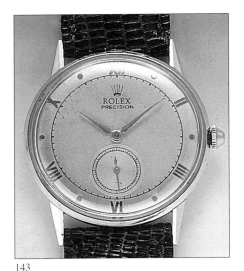

143

144

145

147 A

146

147 B

143 Rolex Precision
Circa 1950. 18-karat yellow gold. No. 3667. Stem-wind. 17 jewels. Breguet hairspring. Superbalance.
(Breitsprecher)　　　$1,050-1,800

144 IWC
Fifties. Steel case. Teardrop attachments. Stem-wind. 12-ligne anchor movement, Caliber 88. 16 jewels. Breguet hairspring. Monometallic screw balance.
(Privately owned.)　　$900-1,170

145 West-End-Watch
Fifties. Pillow-shaped steel case. Stem-wind. Anchor escapement. Flat hairspring. Nickel balance. $180-270
(Privately owned)

146 Omega
Fifties. Yellow gold. Stem-wind. Caliber 265. 15 jewels. Flat hairspring. Glucydur balance. Shock resistance.
(Privately owned)　　　$720-900

147 Vacheron & Constantin
Fifties. 18-karat yellow gold. Stem-wind. Movement no. 507767. Caliber P 1007/BX. 18 jewels. Breguet hairspring. Glucydur balance. Second stopped by crown (stoppable balance).
(Privately owned)　　$2,700-3,150

148 Minerva
Fifties. 18-karat gold. Stem-wind. Central second. Shock resistance.
(Breitsprecher) $540-720

149 Marvin
Fifties. Chrome-plated metal case. Stem-wind. Caliber 360. Direct central second. 15 jewels. Self-compensating hairspring. Glucydur balance.
(Breitsprecher) $450-675

150 Vacheron & Constantin
Fifties. 18-karat gold. Stem-wind. Caliber 406, 9 lignes. 17 jewels. Breguet hairspring. Glucydur balance.
(Mercier) $1,800-2,250

151 Eterna
Fifties. Stainless steel. Stem-wind. Caliber 1020. 15 jewels. Flat hairspring. Glucydur balance.
(Henrys) $270-360

152 Ecole D'Horlogeries, Geneva.
Fifties. Stainless steel. Stem-wind. Patek Philippe caliber 27-400. 18 jewels. Breguet hairspring. Monometallic screw balance. Shock resistance. Fine regulation.
(Privately owned) $3,600-4,500

148

149

150

151

152 A

152 B

153

154

155

156

157 A

157 B

153 LeCoultre
Fifties. Steel case. Stem-wind. (Privately owned) $540-720

154 LeCoultre Coronet
Circa 1952. 10-karat white gold-filled case with striking attachments. Stem-wind. Caliber 480/CW. 17 jewels. Flat hairspring. Screw balance. (Joseph) $450-720

155 Wittnauer
Circa 1952. 14-karat yellow gold. Stem-wind. Movement by Revue, Switzerland, Caliber 76/1. 17 jewels. Flat hairspring. Monometallic screw balance. (Henrys) $270-360

156 Juvenia
Circa 1952. Stainless steel. Model MFG. Stem-wind. 17 jewels. Flat hairspring. Glucydur balance. (Henrys) $270-405

157 Piaget
Circa 1956. 18-karat gold. Stem-wind. 10.5 ligne Eta caliber. 17 jewels. Direct central second. Flat hairspring. Monometallic screw balance. Incabloc shock resistance. (Privately owned) $810-1,080

158 IWC
Circa 1954. Stainless steel. Stem-wind. Caliber 89. 16 jewels. Self-compensating hairspring. Bimetallic balance. Incabloc shock resistance.
(Breitsprecher) $720-1,080

159 Audemars Piguet for Cartier
Circa 1958. 950 platinum. Original platinum band. Stem-wind. Caliber 2001. 18 jewels. Breguet hairspring. Glucydur balance.
(Henrys) $2,700-3,150

160 Zenith Pilot
Circa 1955. Gold-plated. Stem-wind. 12-ligne Caliber 120. 18 jewels. Flat hairspring. Monometallic screw balance. Central second. Balance-stopping apparatus.
(Privately owned) $540-720

161 Audemars Piguet
Late fifties. 18-karat yellow gold. Stem-wind. Caliber 2001, 9 lignes. 18 jewels. Breguet hairspring. Glucydur balance.
(Privately owned) $810-1,080

162 Omikron
1960. Chrome-plated metal case. Black dial, luminous numerals and hands. Hand-wind. Unitas caliber. 21 jewels. Flat hairspring.
(Breitsprecher) $180-225

158

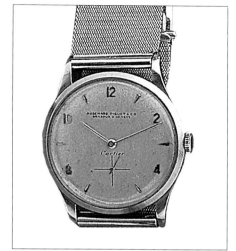

159

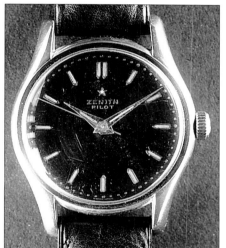

160 A

160 B

161

162

163

164

165

166

167

168

163 Astrolux

Sixties. Gold-plated. Stem-wind. 19 jewels. Flat hairspring. Glucydur balance. Shock resistance.
(Privately owned) $270-315

164 Audemars Piguet

1960. 18-karat yellow gold. Stem-wind. Caliber 2001. 18 jewels. Breguet hairspring. Glucydur balance. Restored dial.
(Privately owned) $2,250-3,150

165 LeCoultre

Circa 1960. 14-karat yellow gold. Calendar. Stem-wind. Caliber 886. Central second. 17 jewels. Flat hairspring. Glucydur balance. Shock resistance.
(Joseph) $810-1,260

166 Ebel

Circa 1964. 18-karat yellow gold. Waterproof. Stem-wind. Caliber 106. 17 jewels. Flat hairspring. Glucydur balance. Shock resistance.
(Henrys) $360-450

167 Rolex "Precision"

Circa 1962. 18-karat yellow gold. No. 9708. Stem-wind. Caliber 1210. 18 jewels. Breguet hairspring. Gyromax balance. KIF shock resistance.
(Breitsprecher) $1,350-2,700

168 Hamilton

Circa 1960. Gold-plated. Screwed bottom. Stem-wind. Caliber 735. 18 jewels. Flat hairspring. Screw balance.
(Breitsprecher) $180-270

169 Longines
Circa 1965. 18-karat yellow gold. Calendar. Stem-wind. Caliber 701. 17 jewels. Flat hairspring. Screw balance. KIF shock resistance.
(Breitsprecher) $360-450

170 Anonymous
1965. Steel case. Regulator dial. Stem-wind. 15 jewels. Central second, small hour and minute.
(Privately owned) $585-720

171 Jules Jürgensen, USA-Switzerland
Circa 1966. 14-karat yellow gold. Stem-wind. 17 jewels. Flat hairspring. Glucydur balance.
(Breitsprecher) $360-450

172 Certina
Circa 1967. Gold-plated. Screwed bottom. Waterproof. Stem-wind. 17 jewels. Flat hairspring. Glucydur balance. Shock resistance.
(Breitsprecher) $180-225

173 Audemars Piguet
Circa 1969. 18-karat yellow gold. No. 44369. Stem-wind. Caliber 2003. 17 jewels. Flat hairspring. Glucydur balance.
(Henrys) $1,800-2,250

169

170

171

172

173

174

175

176 A

176 B

174 Jules Jürgensen, USA-Switzerland
Seventies. 14-karat gold. Stem-wind. 17 jewels. Flat hairspring. Screw balance. Shock resistance.
(Breitsprecher) $460-450

175 Hamilton
1980. Stainless steel case. US Army service watch. Black dial with luminous hands. Stem-wind. Central second. 11.5-ligne caliber. 17 jewels.
(Breitsprecher) $135-225

176 Jean Lassale
As of 1978. 18-karat white gold. Thinnest stem-wind movement ever made. Caliber 1200. 9 jewels. 5 adjustments. Flat hairspring. Glucydur balance. Shock resistance.
(Privately owned) $1,350-1,800

177 Raketa, USSR
1980. Chrome-plated metal case. Stainless steel bottom. 17 jewels. Flat hairspring. Glucydur balance. Shock resistance.
(Henrys) $180-270

177

178

Wristwatches with Automatic Winding

Even though at first glance they usually look similar, wristwatches with automatic winding contain many technical differences. These are the wristwatches with automatic winding that have been built since 1925.

The early self-winding systems of the thirties are actually more curiosities than useful watches today, even though they enjoy great popularity among certain collectors. This raises their prices. But another factor is that functioning examples from that era when the automatic wristwatch was still in its infancy are relatively rare.

Automatic watches from the years after 1940 are also the subjects of numerous collectors' interest. They were made in large numbers and, thanks to their more highly developed designs, generally have preserved their ability to function after many years.

179 A

179 B

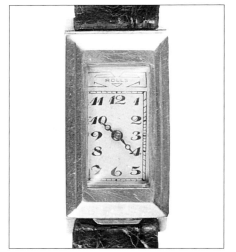

180 A

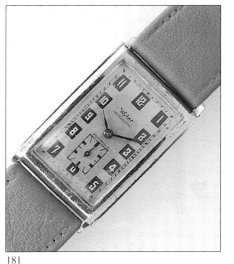

180 B

181

182

178 Patek Philippe

Eighties. 18-karat white gold. Rotor winding. Caliber 77-460 M, 5 adjustments. 37 jewels. Breguet hairspring. Gyromax balance. Shock resistance. Date indication.
(Privately owned) $6,300-7,200

179 Harwood

Late twenties. Silver. Special features: Turn the bezel for hand-setting, red dot shows that power flow between movement and hands is reestablished. Automatic winding by hammer. 10.5-ligne caliber. 15 jewels. Flat hairspring. Compensated balance.
(Privately owned) $720-900

180 Rolls

Early thirties. Gold-plated hinged case. Movement moves in case to cause winding. 5.5-ligne caliber. 17 jewels. Flat hairspring. Bimetallic balance.
(Voithenberg) $720-1,080

181 Wyler

Early thirties. Chrome-nickel hinged case. Crown on the back. Anchor movement. Winding by changes of wrist circumference (moveable bottom). 17 jewels. Flat hairspring. Bimetallic balance.
(Joseph) $720-1,080

182 Wig-Wag for J. Stern, Johannesburg

Thirties. Chrome-plated. Automatic winding. Round anchor movement by Aster. 17 jewels. Flat hairspring.
(Henrys) $720-1,080

183 Perpetual
1935. Gilt case. Automatic with oscillating pendulum. Caliber built by Frey of Biel. Formed anchor movement. 4 adjustments. 15 jewels. Flat hairspring. Bimetallic balance.
(Joseph) $630-810

184 Perpetual
1935. Gold-plated case. Crown to left. Oscillating pendulum. 15 jewels. Flat hairspring. Bimetallic balance.
(Henrys) $630-810

185 Autorist
1935. 9-karat rose gold, side hinge. Automatic winding by changes in wrist dimensions (flexible case lugs). Formed movement 796 by A. Schild S.A. 6.75 lignes. 15 jewels. Flat hairspring. Screw balance.
(Joseph) $720-1,080

186 Omega
Late forties. 18-karat yellow gold. Automatic winding by hammer. Caliber 28.10. 17 jewels. Nivarox hairspring. Compensated balance.
(Breitsprecher) $900-1,080

187 LeCoultre
1848-50. 18-karat gold case. Running reserve indication by the 12. Automatic winding by hammer. Caliber 481. 17 jewels. Breguet hairspring. Screw balance. Superchoc shock resistance.
(Privately owned) $1,080-1,350

188 Movado, Tempomatic
Late forties. Screwed stainless steel case. Automatic winding by hammer. Caliber 220. 17 jewels. Self-compensating hairspring. Compensated balance.
(Breitsprecher) $540-625

183

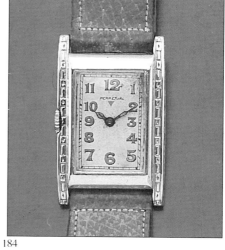

184

185

186

187

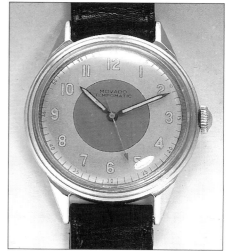

188

189

190

191

192

193 A

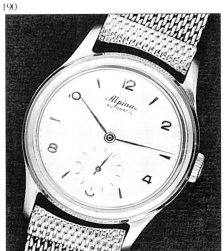

193 B

189 Omega
Late forties. Yellow gold. Running reserve indication at center. Automatic winding by hammer. Caliber 351. 17 jewels. Flat hairspring. Glucydur balance. Incabloc shock resistance.
(Omega) $2,250-2,700

190 Doxa
1950. Steel with red-gold bezel. Central second. Automatic winding by hammer. 11-ligne caliber AS 1250. 17 jewels. Flat hairspring. Monometallic screw balance. Incabloc shock resistance.
(Privately owned) $360-450

191 Wilboi
Fifties. Steel case. Running reserve indication by the 12. Automatic winding by perumtator rotor. 11.5-ligne Felsa 699 caliber. 17 jewels. Flat hairspring. Glucydur balance. Incabloc shock resistance.
(Privately owned) $360-450

192 Alpina
Circa 1950. Stainless steel. Automatic winding by hammer. Caliber 582. 17 jewels. Flat hairspring. Glucydur balance.
(Privately owned) $360-450

193 Movado
Circa 1950. Square gold-filled case. Automatic winding by hammer. Caliber 115, 12 lignes. Round movement. 17 jewels. Flat hairspring. Bimetallic compensated balance. Incabloc shock resistance.
(Voithenberg) $900-1,350

194 Lange

1950. Steel case. Rotor winding. "Bidynator". Felsa 1560 caliber. 17 lignes. Flat hairspring. Bimetallic balance. Incabloc shock resistance. Fine regulation.
(Privately owned) $1,080-1,350

195 Movado Tempomatik

Circa 1950. Gold-plated. Automatic winding by hammer. Caliber 221. 17 jewels. Flat hairspring. Bimetallic balance. Incabloc shock resistance.
(Privately owned) $360-450

196 Junghans

Early fifties. Gold-plated. Running reserve indication at the 6. Rotor winding. Caliber 80/12. 22 jewels. Flat hairspring. Glucydur balance. Shock resistance.
(Privately owned) $315-450

197 IWC

1951. 18-karat gold. Rotor winding. Central second. Caliber 85, 10.5 lignes. 21 jewels. Breguet hairspring. Incabloc shock resistance.
(Privately owned) $1,620-1,800

198 Jaeger LeCoultre "Futurematic"

1953. Stainless steel. Crown on the rear (only for hand-setting). Oscillating pendulum. Caliber 497, 14 lignes. 17 jewels. Flat hairspring. Glucydur balance. Running reserve indication through aperture by the 9. Small second by the 3.
(Privately owned) $1,260-1,440

199 Vacheron & Constantin

Circa 1950. 18-karat yellow gold. Central second. Automatic winding by hammer. No. 494872. Caliber 477/1, 12 lignes. Raw movement by LeCoultre. 17 jewels. Breguet hairspring. Monometallic screw balance.
(Privately owned) $3,600-4,050

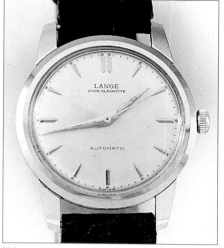

194

195

196

197

198

199

200

201

202

203

204

205

200 LeCoultre Futurematic
1954. 10-karat gold-filled. Crown for hand-setting on the back. Caliber 497. Automatic winding by hammer. 17 jewels. Flat hairspring. Glucydur balance. Shock resistance. Running reserve indication by the 9.
(Privately owned) $1,350-1,620

201 Mondia
Circa 1955. Stainless steel. Running reserve by the 12. Central second. Waterproof. Rotor winding. Caliber AS 1382 N. 17 jewels. Flat hairspring. Glucydur balance. Incabloc shock resistance.
(Henrys) $360-450

202 Longines
Circa 1955. 10-karat yellow gold. Rotor winding. Caliber 19 AS. 17 jewels. Self-compensating flat hairspring. Bimetallic balance. Incabloc shock resistance.
(Breitsprecher) $360-450

203 Omega
1955. 14-karat yellow gold. Rotor winding. Caliber 470. Fine regulation.
(Breitsprecher) $900-1,080

204 Girard Perregaux Gyromatic
1955. Stainless steel. Gold bezel. Caliber 47 EU 753. 17 jewels. Nivarox hairspring. Bimetallic balance. Incabloc shock resistance.
(Privately owned) $540-720

205 Eska
Circa 1955. Stainless steel. Running reserve indication by the 12. Rotor winding. 11.5-ligne Caliber AS 1382. 17 jewels. Flat hairspring. Glucydur balance.
(Privately owned) $360-450

206 Longines Conquest Automatic

1956. Stainless steel. 14-karat gold case. Waterproof. Running reserve indication. Rotor winding. Caliber 294. 24 jewels. Flat hairspring. Glucydur screw balance. Incabloc shock resistance. (Joseph) $1,080-1,440

207 IWC Ingenieur

Mid-fifties. Stainless steel. Calendar. Indirect central second. Rotor winding. 12.75-ligne Caliber 8531. 12 jewels. Breguet hairspring. Monometallic screw balance. Incabloc shock resistance. (Privately owned) $2,700-4,050

208 Omega Seamaster Olympic

1956. 18-karat yellow gold. Rotor winding. Red-gilt anchor movement. Caliber 471. 19 jewels. Breguet hairspring. Glucydur balance. Incabloc shock resistance. (Joseph) $1,800-2,250

209 LeCoultre Automatic

1956. 10-karat gold-filled case. Automatic winding by hammer. 9-ligne Caliber 812. 17 jewels. Flat hairspring. Glucydur balance. Shock resistance. (Henrys) $720-1,080

210 Mido "Multifort"

1958. Stainless steel. Waterproof. "Powerwind" rotor winding. 17 jewels. Nivarox hairspring. Glucydur balance. Incabloc shock resistance. (Breitsprecher) $360-450

211 Eterna

1958. Gold case. Rotor winding. Golden rotor. Caliber 2365. Flat hairspring. Glucydur balance. Shock resistance. World's smallest automatic movement at the time. (A. Bauer) $1,350-1,800

206

207

208

209

210

211

212

213

214

215

216

217

212 Eterna-matic "Centenaire"
Sixties. 18-karat yellow gold. Date indication. Rotor winding with ball bearings. Caliber 1438/U. 21 jewels. Flat hairspring. Self-compensating beryllium balance. Eccentric fine regulation. (Breitsprecher) $540-720

213 Longines "Conquest"
1957. Stainless steel. Waterproof. Calendar. Eccentric automatic winding. Caliber 19 ASD. 19 jewels. Self-compensating hairspring. Glucydur balance. Incabloc shock resistance. (Henrys) $720-900

214 Movado Kingmatic "Subsea"
1960. Stainless steel. Waterproof. Rotor winding. Caliber 531. 28 jewels. Flat hairspring. Bimetallic balance. Incabloc shock resistance. (Privately owned) $450-540

215 Poljot, USSR
1960. Steel case. De Luxe Automatic. Rotor winding. 29 jewels. Flat hairspring. Bimetallic screw balance. Shock resistance. (Privately owned) $270-360

216 Vacheron & Constantin
1960. 18-karat gold. Date indication. Caliber VC PI 1090. Ruby rollers. 21 jewels. 5 adjustments. Breguet hairspring Gyromax balance. Shock resistance. Special feature: 18-karat gold rotor. (Privately owned) $2700-3150

217 Girard Perregaux Gyromatic
Circa 1960. Inverted steel case. Rotor winding. Caliber 21/904. 17 jewels. Self-compensating flat hairspring. Glucydur balance. Incabloc shock resistance.
(Breitsprecher) $360-450

218 Longines Admiral

Circa 1960. 14-karat yellow gold. No. 69 384 A. Rotor winding with toothed ring. Caliber 342. 17 jewels. Glucydur balance. Shock resistance. Pulse-meter scale.
(Joseph) $900-1,080

219 IWC Automatic de Luxe

Circa 1960. 18-karat yellow gold. Central second. Calendar. Rotor winding. 12.75-ligne Caliber 8531. 21 jewels. Breguet hairspring. Incabloc shock resistance.
(Breitsprecher) $900-1,350

220 Omega Seamaster de Ville

Circa 1966. 14-karat gold-filled case. Date. Central second. Waterproof. Rotor winding. Caliber 563. Gilt movement. 17 jewels. Self-compensating flat hairspring. Glucydur balance. Shock resistance. $720-900

221 Jules Jürgensen, Switzerland-USA

Circa 1962. Stainless steel. Waterproof. Rotor winding. Caliber AS 1700. 17 jewels. Flat hairspring. Glucydur balance. Incabloc shock resistance.
(Privately owned) $360-450

222 Rolex Oyster Perpetual

1965. 14-karat gold-filled case. Waterproof. Rotor winding. Caliber 1520. 17 jewels. Nivarox hairspring. Gyromax balance. KIF shock resistance.
(Breitsprecher) $900-1,350

223 Juvenia

1965. Stainless steel. Central second. Rotor winding. Caliber 652-AS 1680. 17 jewels. Incabloc shock resistance. 24-hour indication.
(Privately owned) $540-810

218

219

220

221

222

223

224

225

226

227

228

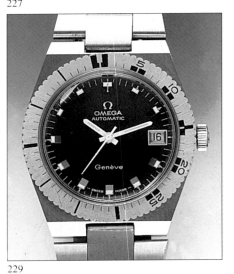

229

224 LeCoultre Master Mariner
Circa 1966. 14-karat yellow gold. Rotor winding. 17 jewels. Flat hairspring. Glucydur balance. Incabloc shock resistance. Day and date indication.
(Henrys) $900-1,080

225 Universal "Polerouter"
1969. Stainless steel. Waterproof. Calendar. Microrotor. Caliber 215/1. 28 jewels. Flat hairspring. Bimetallic balance. Incabloc shock resistance.
(Breitsprecher)   3600-450

226 Rolex Airking Automatic
Circa 1970. Stainless steel. Waterproof screwed crown. Rotor winding. No. 1002. Caliber 1530. Self-compensating flat hairspring. Glucydur balance. KIF shock resistance.
(Breitsprecher) $1,170-1,350

227 Lignal watch for the blind
1970. Nickel. Lifting glass rim. Rotor winding. 11.5-ligne Eta 2784 caliber. 25 jewels. Flat hairspring. Glucydur balance. Shock resistance.
(Privately owned) $360-450

228 Patek Philippe
As of 1979. 18-karat yellow gold. Crown on the rear for hand-setting. Rotor winding. Caliber 1-350. 28 jewels. Breguet hairspring. Gyromax balance. Shock resistance.
(Privately owned) $3,600-4,050

229 Omega Geneve Automatic
1980. Stainless steel. Waterproof. Date indication. Rotating bezel. Rotor winding. Gilt movement. 21 jewels. Self-compensating flat hairspring. Glucydur balance. Shock resistance.
(Breitsprecher) $540-720

230

Waterproof Wristwatches

The name "Rolex" is often associated with waterproof wristwatches. This is correct insofar as this firm put the first truly waterproof wristwatches on the market. There were, however, waterproof cases in existence earlier. Their protection against penetrating dampness was only limited, as their designs were too complicated and depended on too many separate waterproofings. The designs of the twenties, thirties and forties also had specific problems of this kind. As a rule, these watches are no longer waterproof after many years of use, at least not according to the present-day definition. Thus a collection should be limited primarily to the special designs of case types.

231

232

233

234

230 Elgin
Circa 1940. U.S. Navy engraving. 234 C. Stem-wind, screwed-on crown protection. 10-ligne Caliber 539. 16 jewels. Flat hairspring.
(Joseph) $540-720

231 Anonymous, Swiss
Circa 1920. Screwed nickel case. Interior (movement) folds out on hinge. Stem-wind. 15 jewels.
(Joseph) $450-540

232 Rolex Oyster Ultra Prima
Circa 1928. 18-karat yellow gold. Double screwed case. Lead thickening, screwed crown. Stem-wind. Nickel-plated Ultra Prima movement. 15 jewels. 6 adjustments. Compensating hairspring. Bimetallic balance. "Canal-swimmer" model.
(Henrys) $1,350-2,250

233 Rolex Oyster
Circa 1935. 9-karat gold. No. 37216. Screwed crown and movement. Stem-wind. 15 jewels. Breguet hairspring. Superbalance.
(Henrys) $1,350-2,250

234 Rolex Oyster
Circa 1928. Screwed chrome-plated case and crown. Stem-wind. No. 1072. 15 jewels. Breguet hairspring. Bimetallic balance.
(Henrys) $1,080-1,440

235 Omega
Circa 1938. 18-karat yellow gold. Crown by the 12. Sliding case. Stem-wind. 15 jewels. Breguet hairspring. Bimetallic balance.
(Joseph) $1,620-2,250

235 A   235 B   235 C

236 BWC
1940. Stainless steel. Early waterproof case. Stem-wind. Caliber 148 by FEF, 7.75 by 11 lignes. 15 jewels. Breguet hairspring. Geneva stripes. Bimetallic balance.
(Privately owned) $360-630

237 Omega
1940. Stainless steel. Waterproof. Stem-wind. Formed movement, 7.75 by 11 lignes. 15 jewels. Flat hairspring. Bimetallic balance.
(Omega) $720-900

238 Rolex "Marina Militaire"
Circa 1944. Stainless steel case, screwed movement and crown. Stem-wind. 17 jewels. Breguet hairspring. Monometallic screw balance. Italian Navy watch.
(Henrys) $8,100-10,800

239 Laco Sport
1950. V 2 A Krupp stainless steel. Screwed case. Stem-wind. 10.5-ligne movement by Durowe. 16 jewels. Flat hairspring. Incabloc shock resistance.
(Privately owned) $180-270

240 Mido Powerwind
1960. Diver's watch, waterproof to 350 meters. Stainless steel. Rotating bezel. Rotor winding. Dial with decompression scale. (Joseph) $720-900

241 Laco Sport
1950. Stainless steel. Waterproof. Stem-wind. 17 jewels. Glucydur balance. Shock resistance.
(Privately owned) $90-180

236

237

238

239

240

241

242

243

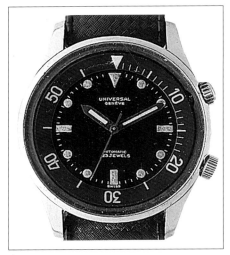

245

246

242 Wittnauer
Circa 1965. Stainless steel. Two crowns to set the inner ring. Rotor winding. Caliber AS 1700. 17 jewels. Flat hairspring. Glucydur balance. KIF shock resistance.
(Breitsprecher) $270-360

243 Zodiac "Seawolf"
Circa 1965. Stainless steel. Rotating bezel. Rotor winding. 17 jewels. Flat hairspring. Glucydur balance. Incabloc shock resistance.
(Breitsprecher) $360-450

244 Universal
Circa 1965. Stainless steel. Screwed jewels. Microrotor winding. 17 jewels. Flat hairspring. Glucydur balance. Incabloc shock resistance. Dial ring turned by crown over the 2.
(Joseph) $540-720

245 Blancpain "Fifty Fathoms Milspec I"
Stainless steel. Black turning bezel. Rotor winding. Basic caliber by AS. Flat hairspring. Glucydur balance. Waterproof to 200 meters. (Privately owned) $1,170-1350

246 Movado HS 288
Stainless steel Mod DEFY. Waterproof. Movado-Zenith caliber. 17 jewels. Flat hairspring. Glucydur balance. Incabloc shock resistance.
(Breitsprecher) $540-630

247 IWC Aquatimer
1970. Stainless steel. Timing ring for diving time set by second crown. Rotor winding. Calendar. 13-ligne Caliber 8541 B. 21 jewels. Breguet hairspring. Glucydur balance. Incabloc shock resistance. Waterproof of 200 meters. Date indication.
(Privately owned) $3,150-4,050

MARINE CHRONOMETER

Constellation

MEGAQUARTZ
ƒ 2,4 MHz

SWISS   MADE

5

Ω   OMEGA

248

Chronometers

A chronometer is a precision clock that is regulated in various positions and at different temperatures, and has received a certificate of accuracy after official tests. The special nature of an officially tested chronometer is that one cannot see its qualities with a loupe. Assuming the caliber is the same, its movement cannot optically be differentiated from an untested specimen. Many firms used to advertise that the movements of their wrist chronometers came from normal series production. This fact naturally resulted in the misuse of the title of "chronometer" on dials. Not every watch that carries this title can therefore show precision regulation in five positions and at three different temperatures, to say nothing of passing an official test over a period of 44 days.

The original precision of chronometers lasts only for a limited time; thus it would be a mistake to buy a veteran wrist chronometer today solely for extreme accuracy. Accurate knowledge should be used when purchasing and collecting chronometers

249

250

251

252

253 A   253 B

248 Omega "Marine Chronometer" Constellation Megaquartz 2.4 Mhz
1972. Stainless steel. Gold bezel. Quartz movement. Caliber 1520. 13 jewels. (Privately owned)$1,080-1,260

249 Rolex Oyster Perpetual Chronometer "Bubble Back"
Circa 1945. Stainless steel. No. 344727, #2940. Rotor winding. 10.5 lignes. 17 jewels. Breguet hairspring. Superbalance. (Henrys) $1,980-2,340

250 Rolex Oyster
1940-50. 18-karat yellow gold. Rotor winding. 17 jewels. Breguet hairspring. Superbalance. With original chronometer certificate and box.
(de Cuellar, Zürich) $3,600-4,050

251 Rolex "Bubble Back"
Circa 1943. Automatic Chronometer. Steel and gold case. #5011. Waterproof. Rotor winding. 18 jewels. Breguet hairspring. Superbalance.
(Breitsprecher) $1,980-.2250

252 Rolex Oyster Imperial for Beyer of Zürich
Circa 1945. Stainless steel. Stem-wind. Extra Prima. 10.5 lignes. 6 adjustments. 18 jewels. Breguet hairspring. Superbalance.
(Privately owned) $1,260-1,440

253 Omega Chronometer
Late forties. Stainless steel. Stem-wind. 13.25-ligne Caliber 30 T(a Rg. 17 jewels. Breguet hairspring. Bimetallic balance.
(Privately owned) $1,800-2,260

254 Eterna-matic Chronometer
Circa 1950. 18-karat yellow gold. Rotor winding. Caliber 1247. 21 jewels. 5 adjustments. Flat hairspring. Monometallic screw balance. Shock resistance.
(Joseph) $720-900

255 Omega Constellation
1952-53. 18-karat yellow gold. Rotor winding. 12.5-ligne caliber 351. 17 jewels. Flat hairspring. Monometallic ring balance. Incabloc shock resistance.
(Breitsprecher) $1,080-1,350

256 Omega Constellation Chronometer
1954. Stainless steel. Waterproof. Rotor winding. Caliber 354. 17 jewels. Flat hairspring. Glucydur balance. Incabloc shock resistance.
(Henrys) $720-1,080

257 Omega Constellation
1965. Stainless steel. Waterproof. Date indication. Rotor winding. Gilt movement. Caliber 561. 24 jewels. Self-compensating flat hairspring. Glucydur balance. Incabloc shock resistance.
(Henrys) $720-900

258 Laco Chronometer
Late fifties. 14-karat yellow gold. Stemwind. Caliber 630 by Durowec. 12 lignes. Direct central second. 21 jewels. Flat hairspring. Beryllium balance. Duroswing shock resistance.
(Privately owned) $450-540

254

255

256

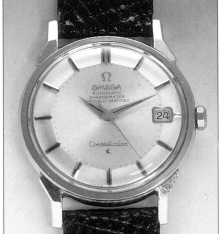

257

258 A

258 B

259 A

259 B

259 Junghans Automatic Chronometer
Mid-sixties. Stainless steel. Date indication. Automatic winding by rotor. 12.5-ligne. Caliber J 83. Direct central second. 29 jewels. Flat Nivarox hairspring. Monometallic ring balance.
(Privately owned) $270-360

260 Junghans Chronometer
Late sixties. Gold-plated case. Stemwind. 12-ligne 82/1, no. 92262. Indirect central second. 17 jewels. Nivarox hairspring. Glucydur balance. Shock resistance.
(Privately owned) $270-360

261 Eterna-matic Chronometer
1968. Stainless steel with gold bezel. Waterproof. Rotor winding. 12.25-ligne Caliber 1414. 21 jewels. Flat hairspring. Glucydur screw balance.
(Henrys) $270-360

262 Ulysse Nardin Chronometer
Seventies. 18-karat yellow gold. Waterproof screwed case. Date indication. Rotor winding. ETA caliber. 25 jewels. Flat hairspring Glucydur balance. Incabloc shock resistance.
(Henrys) $540-720

263 Universal Chronometer
Circa 1970. 18-karat yellow gold. Date indication. Microrotor winding. Caliber 69. Flat hairspring. Glucydur balance. Incabloc shock resistance.
(Breitsprecher) $1,080-1,170

260

262

263

264

Chronographs

Chronographs have enjoyed great popularity among collectors for quite some time. One reason is their functioning, another is their interesting external appearance. As with other types of watches, too, there is a wide variety of designs and quality in their movements, and a famous name does not necessarily indicate that firm's own caliber, or a special one.

In the realm of the chronograph, the number of suitable raw movements has been very limited from the beginning. This means that the same basic caliber can be present in watches of very different price categories. Only the degree of fine workmanship and regulation differentiates one manufacturer's product from another's in many cases. Yet even these differences can disappear, leaving only the name to determine the price.

Before buying a chronograph one should give much consideration to which criteria fits one's personal preference: the year, the condition, the name, the technology, the degree of fine workmanship, the design and/or the case material.

265

266

264 Breitling Chronomat
1945. Stainless steel, rotating bezel for calculation. Tachometer and telemeter scales. Stem-wind. Venus Caliber 175. 17 jewels. Self-compensating hairspring and monometallic balance. Incabloc shock resistance. 45-minute counter. (Privately owned) $1,350-1,620

265 Pavel Buhré
1908-10. Silver. Enameled dial. Caliber by Nicolet. One button by the 12. 60-minute counter. 17 jewels. Breguet hairspring. Bimetallic balance. (Henrys) $1,620-1,800

266 National Park Chronometre
Circa 1928. 18-karat yellow gold hinged case. Stem-wind. 17 jewels. One button. 30-minute counter. Breguet hairspring. Monometallic screw balance. Telemeter and tachometer scales. Restored dial. (Henrys) $1,800-1,980

267 Anonymous
1930. Steel. One button. Stem-wind. 17 jewels. 30-minute counter. Breguet hairspring. Screw balance. Telemeter and tachometer scales. (Privately owned) $572-855

268 Omega
Thirties. Silver. One button. Enameled dial. Stem-wind. Caliber 28.9 T 1. 30-minute counter. 17 jewels. Breguet hairspring. Bimetallic balance. (Omega) $2,250-2,700

267

268

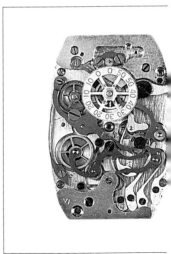

269 A

269 B

269 C

269 Invicta
1935. Stainless steel. Stem-wind. Formed movement. 17 jewels. Breguet hairspring. Hands run backwards. Very unusual watch.
(Voithenberg) $5,400-7,200

270 Gallet
1935. Stainless steel. Stem-wind. Valus Caliber 140, 13-lignes. 30-minute counter. 15 jewels. Flat hairspring. Special feature: Hours and minutes by the 12. (Joseph) $1,350-1,620

271 Patek Philippe
1938. 18-karat gold. Model 1436. Stem-wind. Split second. 25 jewels. Breguet hairspring. Bimetallic balance. 30-minute counter. Tachometer scale in miles.
(Habsburg) $360,000-450,000

272 Doxa
1938. Chrome-plated metal case. Regulator dial. Stem-wind. Venus Caliber 140, 13 lignes. 15 jewels. Flat hairspring. Glucydur balance. Tachometer and telemeter scales.
(Henrys) $450-630

273 Gruen Chonotimer
Forties. Gold-plated. Stem-wind. Caliber 450. 17 jewels. 1 button. Pulse counter.
(Privately owned) $630-720

274 Movado
1939. 18-karat yellow gold. Two-sided chronograph. Stem-wind. 30-minute counter. Very rare watch.
(Christies) $72,000-90,000

270

271

272

273

274 A

274 B

275

276

277

278

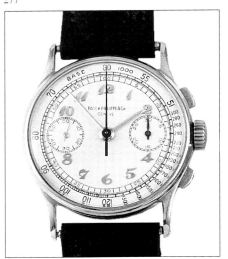

279

280

275 Movado
Late forties. 18-karat gold. Stem-wind. 12-ligne. Movado M 90 caliber. 17 jewels. Breguet hairspring. Glucydur balance. 60 minute counter.
(Voithenberg) $2.250-3.600

276 Pierce
Forties. Stainless steel. Stem-wind. Caliber 130. 17 jewels. Flat hairspring. Glucydur balance. 60-minute counter. Tachometer and telemeter scales.
(Omega) $540-720

277 Bovet
Forties. Single split seconds. Stainless steel. Stem-wind. Valjoux 84 caliber. 17 jewels. Breguet hairspring. Glucydur balance. 30-minute counter. Tachometer and telemeter scales.
(Privately owned) $630-810

278 Doxa "Extra"
Stainless steel. Stem-wind. 17 jewels. 30-minute counter. Tachometer and telemeter scales.
(Antiquorum) $675-855

279 Patek Philippe
Forties. 18-karat gold. Stem-wind. Model 130, 13-ligne Valjoux raw movement. 23 jewels. Breguet hairspring. Glucydur balance. Tachometer scale.]
(Crout) $40.500-54.000

280 Omega
Circa 1942. Stainless steel. Stem-wind. Caliber 27. 17 jewels. Breguet hairspring. Screw balance. Incabloc shock resistance. 30-minute and 12-hour counters. Tachometer scale.
(Breitsprecher) $1.800-2.700

281 Baume & Mercier
1940. 14-karat red gold. 10.5 lignes.
Valjoux 69 caliber. 17 jewels. Breguet
hairspring. Glucydur balance. 30-min-
ute counter. Tachometer scale.
(Antiquorum) $720-900

282 Tissot (Omega)
Forties, Stainless steel. Stem-wind. Gilt
movement. Lemania caliber. 17 jewels.
Breguet hairspring. Screw balance.
30-minute counter. Telemeter and
tachometer scales.
(Breitsprecher) $900-1,080

283 Gallet
Forties. Stainless steel. Stem-wind.
Excelsior Park caliber. 17 jewels. Small
red hand turns once in 24 hours. If one
holds the watch horizontally with the
normal hour hand toward the sun, the
hand with the N will point north.
(Joseph) $540-630

284 Universal
Forties. 18-karat gold. Stem-wind.
Universal caliber. 17 jewels. Breguet
hairspring. Screw balance. Tachometer
scale. Restored dial.
(Privately owned) $1,200-1,980

285 Three Rolex Chronographs
Thirties/forties. All stainless steel. Stem-
wind. Left 13 lignes, middle 14.5, right
10.5 lignes. 17 jewels. Breguet hairspring. Monometallic balance.
(Antiquorum) $9,000-10,800 ea.

281

282

283

284

285 A   285 B   285 C

286

287

286 Movado
Forties. 18-karat gold. Stem-wind. Caliber 95 M. 17 jewels. Breguet hairspring. Glucydur balance. 30-minute and 12-hour counters. Anti-magnetic soft iron capsule.
(Antiquorum) $2,250-2,700

287 Gallet-Decimal
Circa 1940. Stainless steel. Outside decimal scale. Gilt movement. 17 jewels. Breguet hairspring. Monometallic screw balance.
(Joseph) $720-900

288 Angelus
1942. Stainless steel. Stem-wind. Caliber 215. Breguet hairspring. Glucydur balance. 45-minute counter. Tachometer scale.
(Breitsprecher) $540-720

289 Eterna
Forties. Stainless steel. Square case. Stem-wind. Caliber 702, 10.5 lignes. Valjoux 69 basic movement. 17 jewels. Flat hairspring. 30-minute counter.
(Henrys) $540-720

290 Eterna
1943. Stainless steel. With calendar. Stem-wind. Caliber 1068, 13-lignes, Valjoux 72 C basic movement. 17 jewels. Breguet hairspring. Glucydur balance.
(Henrys) $810-990

288

289

290 A   290 B

291 Minerva

Forties. Stainless steel. Screwed case. Stem-wind. Valjoux 72 caliber. Breguet hairspring. Glucydur balance. Shock-resist system. 30-minute and 24-hour counters. Tachometer scale.
(Breitsprecher) $900-1,080

292 Heuer

1944. Gold-plated with stainless steel bottom. Stem-wind. Venus 170 caliber. 17 jewels. Flat hairspring. Monometallic screw balance.
(Henrys) $900-1,080

293 Movado

1945. Stainless steel. Stem-wind. Caliber 478. 17 jewels. No minute counter.
(Privately owned) $900-1,350

294 Gallet

1945. Stainless steel. Stem-wind. Rare formed movement. Excelsior Park 452 caliber. Breguet hairspring. Glucydur balance. 45-minute counter.
(Breitsprecher) $450-720

295 Doxa

Forties. Stainless steel. Stem-wind. Valjoux 23 caliber. 17 jewels. Breguet hairspring. Glucydur balance. 30-minute counter. Telemeter and tachometer scales.
(Breitsprecher) $360-540

296 Audemars Piguet

1943. 18-karat yellow gold. Stem-wind. 13-ligne Valjoux caliber with split seconds. 20 jewels. Breguet hairspring. Glucydur balance. 30-minute and 12-hour counters.
(Henrys) $180,000-270,000

291

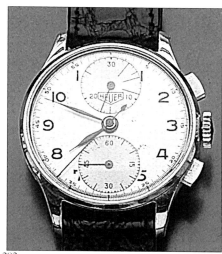

292

293

294

295

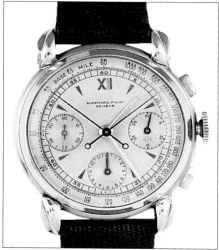

296

297

298

297 Breitling
1950. 18-karat rose gold. Stem-wind. Venus 175 caliber. 17 jewels. Breguet hairspring. Glucydur balance. Supershock-resist system. 45-minute counter. Tachometer scale.
(Breitsprecher) $1,800-2,700

298 GUB (Glashütter Uhrenbetriebe) Fifties. Gold-plated case. Stem-wind. Caliber 64. 17 jewels. 30-minute counter.
(Henrys) $540-720

299 Hanhart
1950. Steel case. Stem-wind. Caliber 41/51. 17 jewels. Breguet hairspring. 30-minute counter.
(Privately owned) $900-1,080

300 Le Phare
1950. Gold-plated. Stem-wind. Valjoux 23 caliber. 17 jewels. Breguet hairspring. Glucydur balance. 30-minute counter. Telemeter and tachometer scales. (Henrys) $720-900

301 Breitling "Premier"
1950. Stainless steel. Stem-wind. Venus 150 caliber. 17 jewels. Breguet hairspring. Glucydur balance. 45-minute counter. Tachometer scale.
(Voithenberg) $720-810

302 Pierce
Circa 1950. Screwed stainless steel case. Stem-wind. Pierce 134 caliber. 17 jewels. Flat hairspring. 60-minute counter.
(Breitsprecher) $450-540

299

300

301

302

303 Angelus Chronodato
Circa 1952. Chrome-plated. Full calendar. Stem-wind. Caliber 217. 17 jewels. 45-minute counter. Breguet hairspring. (Joseph) $1,350-1,620

304 Universal Dato-Compax
1950. Stainless steel. Date. Stem-wind. Universal 285 caliber. 12-hour counter. Tachometer scale.
(Antiquorum) $1,350-1,620

305 Venus
1950. 18-karat red gold. Full calendar and moon phases. Stem-wind. Valjoux 88 caliber. 17 jewels. Breguet hairspring. Glucydur balance. Incabloc shock resistance. Angled and polished steel parts.(Privately owned) $900-1,080

306 Record Split Second
1950. 18-karat gold. Full calendar and moon phases. Stem-wind. Venus 185 split second caliber. 20 jewels. Breguet hairspring. Monometallic screw balance. 30-minute and 12-hour counters. Sweep-hand button in the crown.
(Privately owned) $4,500-5,400

307 Breitling "Duograph"
1950. Steel case. Stem-wind. Venus 179 split second caliber. 20 jewels. Breguet hairspring. Monometallic screw balance. 45-minute counter. Crown serves as sweep-hand button.
(Privately owned) $3,600-5,400

303

304

305 A

305 B

306

307

308

309

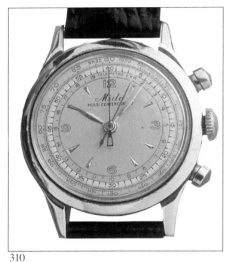

310

311

312

313

308 Anonymous
Fifties. 18-karat yellow gold. Full calendar. Stem-wind. Landeron 180 caliber. 17 jewels. Flat hairspring. Rotating bezel corrects calendar.
(Privately owned) $1,080-1350

309 Orator
Fifties. Stainless steel. Stem-wind. Landeron 815 caliber. 17 jewels. Flat hairspring. Glucydur balance. Full calendar and moon phases.
(Henrys) $1,350-1,620

310 Mido Multicenter
Circa 1955. Screwed stainless case. Stem-wind. Caliber 1300. Gilt movement. 17 jewels. Breguet hairspring. Glucydur balance. Tachometer scale.
(Henrys) $1,080-1,440

311 Wittnauer
Circa 1955. Stainless steel. Stem-wind. Full calendar. Valjoux 72 C caliber. 17 jewels. Breguet hairspring. Glucydur balance. 30-minute and 12-hour counters. Shock resistance.
(Breitsprecher) $1,080-1,350

312 Seafarer
Circa 1955. Stainless steel. Waterproof. Tide indication by the 9. Stem-wind. Valjoux 721 caliber. 17 jewels. Breguet hairspring. Glucydur balance. Incabloc shock resistance. 30-minute and 12-hour counters.
(Breitsprecher) $900-1,360

313 Baume et Mercier
Circa 1954. Screwed stainless steel case. Stem-wind. Landeron 148 caliber. 17 jewels. Flat hairspring. Glucydor balance. Incabloc shock resistance. 45-minute counter.
(Breitsprecher) $720-900

314 Nicolet
1960. Gold-plated. Screwed stainless
steel bottom. Stem-wind. Chronograph
operated by turning the crown. Caliber
251 (Landeron). 17 jewels. Incabloc
shock resistance.
(Joseph) $900-1,080

315 Rolex
18-karat yellow gold. Full calendar.
Stem-wind. Valjoux 72 C caliber.
Breguet hairspring. 30-minute and
12-hour counters.
(Henrys) $18,000-22,500

316 Junghans
1955. Stainless steel. Rotating bezel.
Stem-wind. 14-ligne J 88 caliber. 18
jewels. Breguet hairspring. Glucydur
balance. 30-minute counter.
(Privately owned) $1,080-1,350

317 Movado
1955. Stainless steel. Stem-wind.
12-ligne M 90 caliber. 17 jewels.
Breguet hairspring. Monometallic
screw balance. Special feature: no
small second.
(Privately owned) $1,350-1,800

318 Girard Perregaux
1960. Stainless steel. Stem-wind. 17
jewels. 30-minute and 12-hour counters. (Crott) $540-720

319 Rolex Oyster Cosmograph
1960. Stainless steel. Waterproof.
Screwed buttons and crown. Stem-
wind. 12.5-ligne Valjoux 72 caliber.
19 jewels. Self-compensated balance.
Monometallic balance. 30-minute and
12-hour counters.
(Crott) $12,000-14,000

314

315

316

317

318

319

320

321

322

323

324

325

320 Patek Philippe
Sixties. 18-karat yellow gold. Chronograph with perpetual calendar. #2499. Stem-wind. Movement no. 869336. 13 lignes, rhodinized. Geneva stripes. 23 jewels, 8 adjustments. Breguet hairspring. Glucydur balance. Moon phases. (Privately owned) $180,000-225,000

321 Omega
Circa 1960. 14-karat yellow gold. Stem-wind. Lemania 321 caliber. Self-compensating hairspring and balance. Incabloc shock resistance. 30-minute and 12-hour counters. (Breitsprecher) $1,800-2,250

322 Rolex
1960. 18-karat gold. Stem-wind. Valjoux 72 caliber. 19 jewels. Monometallic screw balance. 30-minute and 12-hour counters. Tachometer scale. (Crott) $16,800-19,800

323 Jaeger LeCoultre
1960. Stainless steel. Rotating bezel with city names. Stem-wind. Valjoux 72 caliber. 17 jewels. Breguet hairspring. Glucydur balance. 30-minute and 12-hour counters. (Privately owned) $1,800-1,980

324 Breitling "Navitimer Cosmonaute"
1965. Stainless steel. #809. Rotating bezel calculator. Stem-wind. Red-gilt anchor movement. Caliber V 178 (Venus). 17 jewels. Flat hairspring. Glucydur balance. 30-minute and 12-hour counters. (Joseph) $2,250-2,700

325 Mathey Tissot
Circa 1965. Rotating bezel, screwed stainless steel case. Valjoux caliber. Stem-wind. 17 jewels. Self-compensating hairspring and Glucydur balance. Shock resistance. Luminous hands and numerals. 30-minute and 12-hour counters. (Joseph) $1,350-1,800

326 Breitling
1965. Stainless steel. Rotating bezel. 765. Stem-wind. Caliber V 178 (Venus). 17 jewels. Flat hairspring. Glucydur balance. Shock resistance. Luminous hands and numerals. Digital 5-minute counter in aperture by the . 12-hour counter.
(Joseph) $1,350-1,800

327 Progress
1970. Gold-plated. Stem-wind. Lanceron 248 caliber. 17 jewels. Breguet hairspring. Glucydur balance. Incabloc shock resistance. 30-minute counter. Telemeter and tachometer scales.
(Breitsprecher) $360-540

328 Breitling
1970. Stainless steel. Waterproof. Stem-wind. 14-ligne basic work, Valjoux 7731 caliber. 17 jewels. Flat hairspring. Shock resistance. Aperture over the 6 shows whether chronograph is switched on
(Privately owned) $450-540

329 Universal Space Compax
Stainless steel. Screwed crown and buttons. Stem-wind. Valjoux 72 caliber. Rotating bezel. 30-minute and 12-hour counters.
(Crott) $900-1,080

330 Zenith, El Primero
Circa 1972. Stainless steel. Calendar. Rotor winding. 13-ligne 3019 PHC caliber. 31 jewels. Flat hairspring. Glucydur balance. Shock resistance. Fast beat escapement. 30-minute and 12-hour counters. Tachometer scale.
(Breitsprecher) $1,080-1,350

331 Heuer
Circa 1975. Screwed waterproof stainless steel case, adjustable bezel. Rotor winding. Heuer 12 caliber. 17 jewels. Flat hairspring. Glucydur balance. Shock resistance. Date, 30-minute and 12-hour counters. Pulse and tachometer scales.
(Henrys) $540-900

326

327

328

329

330

331

332

333

334

335

336

337

332 Wittnauer

Circa 1960. Stainless steel. Waterproof. Venus 188 caliber. 17 jewels. Breguet hairspring. Glucydur balance. Shock resistance. 30-minute counter. Telemeter and tachometer scales.
Breitsprecher) $900-1,080

333 Omega Speedmaster

Chronometer made for Omega's 125th anniversary. Circa 1975. Stainless steel. Rotor winding. Caliber 1041. 13.75 lignes. 17 jewels. Self-compensating flat hairspring. Monometallic ring balance. Shock resistance. 30-minute and 12-hour counters. Tachometer scale. (Privately owned) $720-1,080

334 Omega Seamaster

1976. Stainless steel. Waterproof. Stem-wind. Lemania caliber. 17 jewels. Flat hairspring. Glucydur balance. Incabloc shock resistance. 30-minute and 12-hour counters. Tachometer scale. (Breitsprecher) $630-890

335 Movado Datochron

1975. Hard-gilt metal case. Screwed stainless steel bottom. Rotor winding. Zenith 3019 PHC caliber. Fast beat escapement. 17 jewels. Flat hairspring. Glucydur balance. Shock resistance. Date, 30-minute and 12-hour counters. Tachometer scale. (Breitsprecher) $720-900

336 Heuer Autavia

1975. Stainless steel. Rotor winding. Heuer 12 caliber. 17 jewels. Flat hairspring. Glucydur balance. Shock resistance. Date indication. 30-minute and 12-hour counters. Tachometer scale. (Breitsprecher) $720-900

337 Lemania Regatta

1975. Stainless steel. Rotor winding. 17-jewels. Flat hairspring. Glucydur balance. Shock resistance. Counter for exact regatta starts.
(Joseph) $540-720

338 Breitling Navitimer

1975. Stainless steel. Stem-wind. 14-ligne Valjoux 7740 caliber. 17 jewels. Flat hairspring. Monometallic ring balance. Incabloc shock resistance. 30-minute and 12-hour counters. Date indication. Calculator scale.
(Privately owned) $1,080-1,800

339 Ekegren

1980. 18-karat gold. Rotor winding. Full calendar. 13-ligne Zenith "El Primero" 3019 PHC caliber. 31 jewels. Flat hairspring. Glucydur balance. Fast beat escapement. Incabloc shock resistance. 30-minute and 12-hour counters. Pulse scale.
(Crott) $2,700-3,600

340 Mikado

Circa 1980. Stainless steel. Screwed bottom. Date. Rotor winding. 11.5-ligne Kelek TDBK 1369 caliber. 17 jewels. Flat hairspring. Glucydur balance. Incabloc shock resistance. Module chronograph. 30-minute and 6-hour counters. Pulse scale.
(Breitsprecher) $270-360

341 Omega Speedmaster

1975. Stainless steel. Day date. Waterproof screwed case. Rotor winding. Lemania 5100 caliber. 17 jewels. Flat hairspring. Glucydur balance. Incabloc shock resistance. 30-minute and 12-hour counters, pulse scale.
(Breitsprecher) $720-900

342 Dubey und Schaldenbrand

1985. Gold-plated. "Index Mobile" sweep-hand mechanism, patented 1948. Landeron 51 caliber. 17 jewels. Flat hairspring. Glucydur balance. 30-minute counter.
(Henrys) $720-900

338

339

340

341

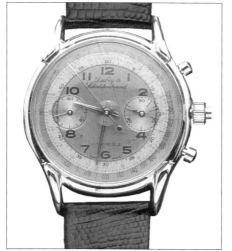

342

343

Calendar Watches

There probably is no other type of wristwatch with such a broad spectrum of different designs, complications and qualities as the calendar watches. The selection ranges from models with manually switched date indication to watches with "perpetual" calendars. Naturally the price usually rises along with the array of complications. But the name of the manufacturer also plays a decisive role in setting the price. So it may well happen that one pays a good deal more for a simple calendar watch by one of the well-known producers of luxury watches than for the perpetual calendar watch of a less renowned producer.

The following calendar indications occur in wristwatches:

Date (hand or aperture), weekday and date (hands and/or apertures), weekday, date and month (hands and/or apertures, the latter manually changeable or automatically switched). All of these indications are also available along with moon-phase indication.

343 Orator

Circa 1956. 18-karat yellow gold. Corrector button in case rim. Stem-wind. Valjoux 90 caliber. 17 jewels. Flat hairspring. Glucydur balance. Incabloc shock resistance. Central second. Full calendar. Moon phases.
(Henrys) $540-720

344 Anonymous

1915. Burnished steel case. Enameled dial, luminous numerals and hands. Stem-wind. 15 jewels. Flat hairspring. Monometallic screw balance.
(Privately owned) $540-720

345 Henry Moser

Circa 1916. Silver. Hand-setting button by the 4. Stem-wind. 16 jewels. Breguet hairspring. Compensated balance. Date and day indication.
(Privately owned) $2,250-3,150

346 Gübelin/AP

1924. 18-karat yellow gold. Stem-wind. Swiss bridge caliber. 18 jewels. Breguet hairspring. 7 adjustments. Bimetallic screw balance. Simple full calendar and moon phases.
(Privately owned) $9,000-13,500

347 Medana

Circa 1928. Hinged chrome-plated case. Second disc turns on itself. Stem-wind. Gilt cylinder movement. Luminous numerals and hands. Date indication in aperture.
(Henrys) $540-720

348 Patek Philippe

1937. 18-karat yellow gold. Model 96. 11-ligne ebauche by V. Piguet, no. 860183. 17 jewels. Breguet hairspring. Bimetallic compensated balance. Perpetual calendar, retrograde date indication.
(Patek Philippe, Geneva)
$720,000-810,000

344

345

346 A

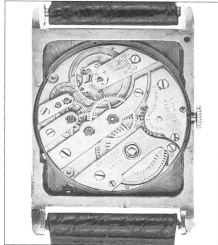

346 B

347

348

349

350

351 A

351 B

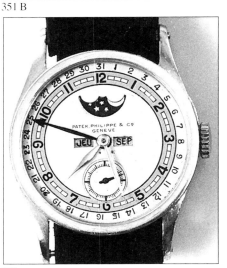

352

353

349 Vibra
Thirties. Chromed nickel case. Stem-wind. Rosskopf movement with pin lever. 7 jewels. Flat hairspring. Special feature: The manually adjustable day (above) the date (below) indications are in the drums of the band attachments. (Antiqorum) $630-810

350 Rolex Perpetual
Circa 1945. Stainless steel. No. 8171/988. Rotor winding. 17 jewels. Breguet hairspring. Superbalance. Full calendar and moon phases.
(Henrys) $10,800-12,600

351 A & B Movado Calendograph
Circa 1939. Stainless steel. Simple full calendar. Stem-wind. Caliber 475. 15 jewels. Breguet hairspring. Screw balance. Indirect central second.
(Privately owned) $720-1,080

352 Record Watch
1940. 18-karat. Full calendar. Stem-wind. Caliber 107, 10.5 lignes. 17 jewels. Flat hairspring. Monometallic screw balance. Moon phase indication.
(Privately owned) $1,800-1,980

353 Patek Philippe
Circa 1937. Platinum. #96. Stem-wind. No. 198297. 11-ligne Vic. Piguet ebauche, second quality. 18 jewels. Flat hairspring. Bimetallic balance.
(Ineichen) $720,000-1,080,000

54 Anonymous
Circa 1945. Stainless steel. Stem-wind. 17 jewels. Self-compensating flat hairspring. Monometallic screw balance. Incabloc shock resistance.
(Privately owned) $360-450

55 LeCoultre
Circa 1947. 10-karat gold-filled case. Stem-wind. Formed anchor movement, 486 AW. 17 jewels. Flat hairspring. Monometallic screw balance. Full calendar, moon phases.
(Joseph/Eder) $3,150-3,600

56 Universal
Circa 1946. 18-karat yellow gold. Stem-wind. Caliber 291. 15 jewels. Breguet hairspring. Bimetallic balance. Full calendar, moon phases.
(Breitsprecher) $2,250-3,150

57 Omega
Circa 1946. Steel with gold bezel. Stem-wind. Caliber 27. 17 jewels. Flat hairspring. Bimetallic balance. Incabloc shock resistance. Full calendar, moon phases.
(Breitsprecher) $2,520-3,150

58 Gübelin
Circa 1948. Stainless steel. Stem-wind. Valjoux caliber. 15 jewels. Self-compensating flat hairspring. Monometallic screw balance. Full calendar.
(Joseph) $1,080-1,350

59 Angelus
Circa 1948. 10-karat gold-filled case. Day (aperture), date and moon phase indication. Stem-wind. Caliber 253. 16 jewels. Flat hairspring. Bimetallic balance.
(Breitsprecher) $540-720

354

355

356

357

358

359

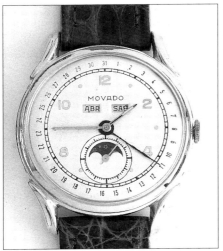

360

361

362

363

364

365

360 Movado
Circa 1949. 18-karat gold. Corrector button on side of case. Stem-wind. Caliber 473. 15 jewels. Flat hairspring. Glucydur screw balance. Full calendar. (Henrys) $1,440-1,620

361 Mido Multifort Datometer
Circa 1955. Screwed stainless steel case. Automatic winding by hammer. 17 jewels. Flat hairspring. Glucydur screw balance. Incabloc shock resistance. Fine regulation. Date shown by central hand.
(Henrys) $360-450

362 Cornavin
1952. Gold-plated case, screwed stainless steel bottom. Day indication by wandering sun in aperture by the 12. 10 lignes. 17 jewels. Date indication. (Joseph) $540-720

363 Crawford, Great Britain
Circa 1950. 9-karat yellow gold. Crown by the 10 to adjust moon aperture and date ring. Stem-wind. Swiss caliber. 17 jewels. (Joseph) $450-720

364 Movado for Tiffany, New York
Circa 1950. Steel case. Corrector button by the 4. Automatic winding by hammer. Caliber 268, 11.5 lignes. 17 jewels. Flat hairspring. Bimetallic balance. Incabloc shock resistance. Day and date indication.
(Privately owned) $1,080-1,350

365 Cornavin, Datocor
1955. Gold-plated. Date by two discs in aperture. Stem-wind. Caliber 221 by Venus, 11.5 lignes. 17 jewels. Flat hairspring. Monometallic screw balance. (Privately owned) $360-540

366 Movado

Stainless steel. Automatic winding by hammer. Caliber 223 A, 12.75 lignes. 17 jewels. Breguet hairspring. Monometallic screw balance. Incabloc shock resistance. Complete simple calendar. (Privately owned) $540-720

367 Dom Watch

Gold-plated. Rotor winding. Four corrector buttons. 17 jewels. Flat hairspring. Glucydur balance. Full calendar, moon phases. (Privately owned) $450-630

368 Henri Duvoisin

Fifties. Gold-plated case. Stem-wind. 17 jewels. Flat hairspring. Glucydur balance. Shock resistance. Full calendar and moon-phase indication. (Privately owned) $450-630

369 Audemars Piguet

Circa 1960. 18-karat yellow gold. Stem-wind. Caliber V 7 SS, 13 lignes. 18 jewels. Breguet hairspring. Monometallic screw balance. Perpetual calendar with moon phases. Leap-year indication. (Privately owned)
$27,000-36,000

370 Gübelin

18-karat yellow gold. Four buttons for correction of day, date, month, moon phases. Rotor winding. "Ipso-matic." 17 jewels. Flat hairspring. Glucydur balance. (Privately owned) $2,250-2,700

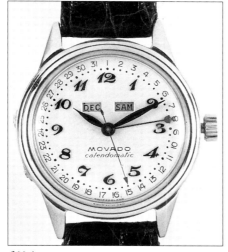

366 A

366 B

367

368

369

370

371

World-Time Watches

Around 1880, the time-table difficulties of the American railways inspired railroad engineer Sandford Flemingo to suggest that the world be divided into 24 time zones. At every fifteen degrees of longitude the time should change by one hour. As of 1883, Flemings idea and, with it, our present-day world time system, became a reality. The watch industry met this time problem by producing watches that indicated two or more zonal times simultaneously, and/or bore a world-time scheme on their dials. Such wristwatches are gathered here under the collector's term of "World-Time Watches."

371 Edox "Geoscope"
Circa 1970. Waterproof steel case. Inner world map turns once in 24 hours. The winding, hand-setting and world-time-setting crowns are on the left side. Very rare watch.
(A. Bauer) $1,080-1,350

372 Louis Cottier Garouge
1950. Pre-series model of world-time watch by Patek Philippe, Geneva. 18-karat gold. Hand-setting by the 3, place-name turning crown by the 9. 12 lignes. 17 jewels. Breguet hairspring. Bimetallic balance.
(Privately owned)$45,000-60,000

373 Patek Philippe
1961. World-time watch after a patent by Louis Cottier. 18-karat white gold. Rotor winding. Caliber 27-460. 37 jewels. Breguet hairspring. Gyromax balance. Shock resistance. Second zonal time is read by using the crown and the button over the crown simultaneously. Very rare watch.
(Patek Philippe, Geneva)
$36,000-45,000

374 Patek Philippe
Circa 1937. 18-karat gold. Model 542. Stem-wind. 10-ligne movement, no. 82 1239. 18 jewels. Flat hairspring. Bimetallic balance.
(Sothebys) $900,000-1,350,000

375 Wyler Incaflex Worldtime
Circa 1958. Stainless steel. Rotating bezel. AS 1361 N automatic movement. 17 jewels. Flat hairspring. Glucydur balance.
(Joseph) $450-630

376 Movado World Time
Steel case. (Joseph) $1,080-1,350

377 Tissot Navigator
1957. 18-karat gold. The inner disc with the city names turns once in 24 hours. Automatic winding by swinging pendulum. Caliber 28.5 N 21, 12.5 lignes. 17 jewels. Flat hairspring. Glucydur balance. Incabloc shock resistance.
(Privately owned) $1,080-1,350

372

373

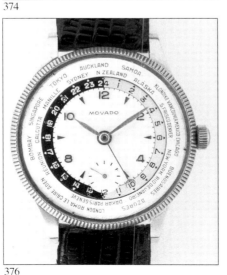

374

375

376

377

378 A

378 B

379

380

381

382

378 Arctos, Horometer, EXSTO System

Fifties. Gold-plated. 11.5-ligne automatic Felsa 790 caliber. 22 jewels. Flat hairspring. Glucydur balance. Shock resistance.
(A. Bauer) $540-720

379 Breitling "Unitime"

Circa 1958. Plaqué case. No. 1-260. Red-gilt automatic movement, Felsa 260 caliber. 21 jewels. Flat hairspring. Glucydur balance. Incabloc shock resistance. Rotating bezel. Date indication by the 3.
(Joseph/JX) $1,620-1,980

380 Ardath "Long Distance"

Sixties. Gold-plated case. Calendar by the 9. Stem-wind and automatic movements: ETA 2551 and FEF 430. Both 17 jewels. Flat hairspring. Glucydur balance. Incabloc shock resistance.
(Privately owned) $720-1,080

381 Enicar Sherpa-Jet

Circa 1965. Steel case. Rotor winding. Date indication. 24-hour hand and rotating bezel.
(A. Bauer) $720-1,080

382 Paul Garnier

Circa 1975. Gilt steel case. Stem-wind. Durowe 391 caliber. 17 jewels. Flat hairspring. Glucydur balance. Duroshock shock resistance.
(Breitsprecher) $360-450

383

Alarm Wristwatches

The alarm is the oldest additional function of the wheel clock. It was first used in a wrist-watch as early as 1908, but became widespread only as of 1947. In the mid-fifties the alarm feature was first put on the market, along with automatic winding. Along with the classic alarm watches, there are also wristwatches with an elapsed-time alarm. These are meant to remind one of expired parking time or some other short period.

384 A

384 B

385

386

387

388

383 LeCoultre Memodate
Circa 1960. Stainless steel. Three crowns: alarm by the 2, turning ring by the 3, winding and hand-setting by the 4. Automatic movement. 17 jewels. Flat hairspring. Glucydur balance. Shock resistance.
(Joseph) $2,700-3,150

384 Junghans Minivox
1949. Stem-wind. Caliber 89, 12.5 lignes. Indirect central second. 20 jewels. Flat hairspring. Glucydur balance. Shock resistance. Alarm crown by the 2, shut-off button by the 4.
(Privately owned) $360-450

385 LeCoultre Memovox
Circa 1954. 10-karat gold-filled case. Stem-wind. Two crowns for time and alarm. Caliber 489. 17 jewels. Flat hairspring. Glucydur balance.
(Breitsprecher) $900-1,080

386 LeCoultre Memovox
1955. Alarm watch with world-time disc. 10-karat gold-filled case. Stem-wind. Caliber 484. 17 jewels. Flat hairspring. Glucydur balance. Shock resistance. (Breitsprecher) $900-1,080

387 Vulcain Cricket
Circa 1960. Stainless steel. Waterproof. Stem-wind. Caliber 120. 17 jewels. Flat hairspring. Monometallic screw balance. Two barrels, for time and alarm, via one crown.
(Privately owned) $360-450

388 Poljot, USSR
Sixties. Steel case. Stem-wind. Caliber 2612 (copy of AS 1475), 11.5 lignes. 18 jewels. Flat hairspring. Nickel balance. Shock resistance.
(Privately owned) $270-360

389 Tudor Advisor

Sixties. Stainless steel. Central second. Stem-wind. 11.5-ligne caliber by AS. 17 jewels. Flat hairspring. Glucydur balance. Shock resistance.
(Privately owned) $270-360

390 Framont

Sixties. Steel case. Elapsed-time alarm to 2 hours. Stem-wind. Venus 232 caliber, 12.5 lignes. 17 jewels. Flat hairspring. Monometallic screw balance. Incabloc shock resistance.
(Privately owned) $360-450

391 Jaeger LeCoultre Memovox

Sixties/seventies. Steel case. Date indication. Rotor winding. Caliber 825, 14 lignes. 17 jewels. Flat hairspring. Glucydur balance. Shock resistance.
(Privately owned) $1,440-1,800

392 Dunhill, Great Britain, made by LeCoultre

18-karat gold. Date indication. Central second. Rotor winding. Caliber 825. 17 jewels. Flat hairspring. Glucydur balance. KIF shock resistance.
(Privately owned) $1,080-1,260

393 LeCoultre Memovox

Late seventies. Stainless steel. Rotor winding. Date indication. Caliber LC 916. Flat hairspring. Glucydur balance. KIF shock resistance. Two barrels for time and alarm.
(Breitsprecher) $720-1,350

394 Omega Seamaster Memomatic

1970. Stainless steel. Rotor winding. Caliber SL 980. 13.5 lignes. 19 jewels. Flat hairspring. Glucydur balance. Shock resistance. One barrel for time and alarm. Alarm can be set to the minute.
(Privately owned) $900-1,080

389

390

391

392

393

394

Repetition Watches

A wristwatch with minute repeat is surely the glory of any collection. Some 300 parts, all carefully prepared and tuned to each other, are required so that the hours, quarter hours and minutes can be indicated acoustically after a small lever is moved. But there are also wristwatches with less impressive striking apparatus, for example, for hours and quarter-hours or for hours and five-minute intervals.

Since the introduction of the electric light, repeat watches - although worthy of admiration - are regarded as anachronisms. For that reason, the number of wristwatches with this complication has always been small. But market development after 1983 has resulted, in particular, in ladies' pocket watches with minute or quarter-hour repeat being rebuilt as wristwatches. This does not undermine the watchmaker's achievement, but does lower the price. Before making a purchase, one should very carefully check the authenticity of such a watch.

395 Golay fils & Stahl

Circa 1920. 18-karat yellow gold. Case probably made later. Stem-wind. LeCoultre caliber. 29 jewels. Breguet hairspring. Compensated balance. Minute repeat lever by the 8. Stem-setting via crown and button by the 4. (Privately owned) $18,000-22,500

396 A & B Hunt & Roskell. Circa

1900. Case circa 1980. 18-karat yellow gold. Stem-wind. Caliber no. 12540. Breguet hairspring. Bimetallic balance. 3 screwed chatons. Quarter-hour repeat. (Privately owned) $6,300-8,100

397 Audemars Piguet

1909, sold 1929. Platinum. Stem-wind. 11.5-ligne SMV caliber. 29 jewels. Flat hairspring. Bimetallic balance. Lever by the 9. Minute repeat. (Ineichen, Zürich) $45,000-54,000

398 Gübelin

1920-1930. Platinum. Silver dial with yellow gold markings. Stem-wind. 9.25 lignes. No. 5802, caliber by LeCoultre. 3 mm high. 29 jewels. Breguet hairspring. Compensated balance with gold screws. Minute repeat. (Gübelin, Lucerne) $31,500-45,000

399 A,B,C Driva Repeater

Circa 1935. 18-karat gold. Stem-wind. Formed movement. 15 jewels. Flat hairspring. Bimetallic balance. Lever between 1 and 2. Quarter repeat. (Privately owned) $5,850-6,750

396 A

396 B

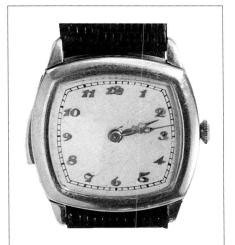

397

398

399 A

399 B

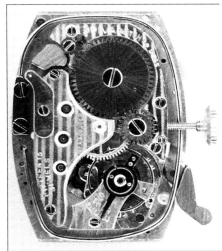

399 C

400 A

401

403

400 B

402

404

400 B. C. Wenger
Circa 1925. White gold. Stem-wind. 10.5 lignes. 29 jewels. Breguet hairspring. Bimetallic balance. Lever by the 9. Minute repeat.
(Sabrier) $31,500-45,000

401 Audemars Piguet
Circa 1945. Platinum. Stem-wind. 11 lignes. 29 jewels. Breguet hairspring. Compensated balance. Lever by the 9. Minute repeat. (Antiquorum)
$54,000-72,000

402 Patek Philippe for Gübelin
Circa 1950-60. 18-karat yellow gold. Stem-wind. 12 lignes. 29 jewels. Breguet hairspring. Bimetallic balance. Lever by the 9. Minute repeat.
(Christies) $162,000-180,000

403 Angelus Tinkler
1957-58. Steel case. Rotor winding. Caliber AS 1580, 11.5 lignes. 17 jewels. Flat hairspring. Monometallic screw balance. Incabloc shock resistance. Special feature: only 100 watches built as pre-series. Lever by the 9. Quarter-hour repeat.
(Sothebys) $3,600-4,500

404 Angelus
Circa 1960. Gold-plated. Stem-wind. Caliber ETA 2801. 17 jewels. Flat hairspring. Glucydur balance. Shock resistance. Button by the 2 to turn off 5-minute repeat.
(Privately owned) $2,700-3,150

405

Various Watches

Since wristwatches have existed, the industry has made an effort to make these timepieces attractive by using unconventional case forms and/or additional functions. Thus the spectrum is incredibly broad. It ranges from the curious Mickey Mouse watch with a simple pin lever movement to the technical refinement of the tourbillon. The watches gathered here are those that would be hard to fit into the previous categories.

406

407

408

409

410

405 Hebdomas
Circa 1918. Hinged metal case. Gilt bezel. Enameled dial with visible screw balance. Stem-wind. Breguet hairspring. Red 12. Eight-day watch.
(Privately owned) $540-720

406 Vacheron & Constantin for Verger, Paris
Twenties. 18-karat white and yellow gold. Dial covered by jalousie. Stem-wind. 9 lignes. 15 jewels. Breguet hairspring. Bimetallic balance. Left crown to open and close jalousies.
(Privately owned) $4,500-5,400

407 Hebdomas Eight-Day Watch
Circa 1920. Nickel. 14 lignes. Breguet hairspring. Screw balance. Large barrel for eight-day movement.'
(Privately owned) $720-900

408 Longines, various pilots' watches
Circa 1930. Stainless steel. Stem-wind.
(Privately owned) $720-3,150

409 Longines, small version of Lindbergh hour-angle watch
1940. 10-karat gold-filled case. Stem-wind. Caliber 10. 15 jewels. Breguet hairspring. Glucydur screw balance. Crown by the 2 for inner disc.
(Joseph) $2,160-2,700

410 LeCoultre
Forties. Stainless steel. Pilot's watch. Stem-wind. Rotating bezel stopped by crown by the 4. 17 jewels. Shock resistance.
(Joseph) $900-1,350

411 Protona
Circa 1940. Stainless steel case with built-in microphone. No movement. So-called "espionage watch." (Joseph) $720-900

412 Longines "Flyback"
Circa 1944. 10-karat gold-filled case. Stem-wind. Caliber 12.687. 17 jewels. Central second and minute, "stop second." (Joseph) $2,250-4,500

413 Juvenia with calculator
1950. Stainless steel. Rotating bezel for calculation. 17 jewels. Self-compensating flat hairspring. Monometallic screw balance. Incabloc shock resistance. (Joseph) $720-900

414 Hamilton "Electric Pacer"
Fifties. Gold-plated. Electrodynamic balance. Caliber 500. 12 jewels. (Privately owned) $540-720

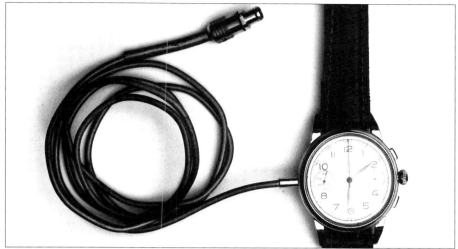

411

412

413

414 A

414 B

415

416

417

418

419

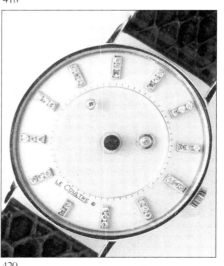

420

415 Players "Soccer Watch"

Circa 1950. Nickel-plated brass case. Stem-wind. 12-ligne FHF 27 caliber. Geneva stripes. 17 jewels. Flat hairspring. Screw balance. The 4 buttons allow scorekeeping for 2 teams.
(Privately owned) $900-1,080

416 Ernest Borel "Cocktail"

Circa 1960. Stainless steel. Stem-wind. The arbor for the central second hand drives a disc that, along with other discs connected to the hour and minute hands, forms kaleidoscope-like pictures. Indirect central second. Incabloc shock resistance.
(Privately owned) $540-720

417 Juvenia

1955. Gold-plated. Time indication by ruler and protractor. Stem-wind. Caliber $ 465. 5 adjustments. 17 jewels. Flat hairspring. Monometallic screw balance.
(Joseph) $1,080-1,350

418 Longines "Mysterieuse"

1958. 18-karat white gold. Diamond-studded bezel and hands. Stem-wind. Caliber 19.4. 17 jewels. Flat hairspring. Glucydur balance. Incabloc shock resistance. Without jewels on the bezel.
$1,350-1,800
With jewels on the bezel
(Joseph) $1,800-1,980

419 Girard Perregaux "Mysterieuse"

Circa 1959. 18-karat yellow gold. Hour and minute indication on turning discs. 17 jewels. Shock resistance.
(Joseph) $720-1,080

420 LeCoultre/Vacheron & Constantin

Circa 1955. 14-karat white gold. Stem-wind. Caliber 480 CW. 17 jewels. "Mysterieuse" watch. Time indication by turning discs.
(Joseph) $2,250-2,700

421 Gruen Airflight, USA
Circa 1960. Stainless steel. Jumphour precision. Central second. Stem-wind. Caliber N 510 SS, 11.5 lignes. 17 jewels. Automatically switches from 1-12 to 13-24 at 1:00 p.m.
(Privately owned) $720-900

422 Favre-Leuba-bivouac
1963. Stainless steel. Stem-wind. Peseux 320 caliber, 10.5 lignes. 17 jewels. Incabloc shock resistance. Includes altimeter (0-3000 meters). Barometer case attached to movement.
(Privately owned) $630-810

423 Doxa
Circa 1960. Stainless steel. Hour indication by sun and moon. Stem-wind. Chézard 116 caliber. 17 jewels. Flat hairspring. Glucydur balance. Springing second.
(Joseph) $450-630

424 Bulova "Spaceview"
1965. Screwed stainless steel case. Crown on back. Battery-powered tuning-fork watch.
(Privately owned) $720-900

425 Le Phare
Circa 1965. Stainless steel. Date. Retrograde time indication (hours, minutes). Peseux 7046 caliber, 10.5 lignes. 17 jewels. Flat hairspring. Glucydur balance. Date indication by the 6.
(Privately owned) $270-360

426 Cervine Masonic Watch
Circa 1960. Gold - plated case. Stem-wind. Cyma 120 caliber. 17 jewels.
(Privately owned) $360-540

421

422

423

424

425

426

427

428

427 Corona Watch, Swiss

Seventies. Chrome-plated metal case. Stem-wind. **EB** pin lever movement.
(Privately owned) $180-270

428 Waltham

Circa 1950. Triangular gold-plated case. Dial with Masonic symbols. Central second. Caliber 25/40. 17 jewels. Shock resistance.
(Privately owned) $1,080-1,350

429 Longines Comet

1972. Stainless steel, waterproof. Stem-wind. Caliber 702. 17 jewels. Self-compensating flat hairspring. Ring balance. Shock resistance. "Mysterieuse." Two discs with dots and arrows replace the hands.
(Joseph) $270-450

430 Heuer Solunar

19875. Stainless steel. Rotor winding. Day and date indication plus tide indication, which must be set manually every 14 days.
(Privately owned) $540-900

431 Omega 300 Hz Tuning-Fork Chronometer

1976. Stainless steel. Battery-powered movement.
(Breitsprecher) $360-540

432 Ernest Borel Cocktail Watch

Circa 1978. Waterproof gilt metal case. Rotor winding. 17 jewels. Self-compensating hairspring and balance. Shock resistance. Turning discs form a constantly changing pattern in which hands appear.
(Breitsprecher) $180-315

433 Swatch

Pop art, 1991, "GU(H)RKE" by Alfred Hofkunst, Vienna $540-720

429

430

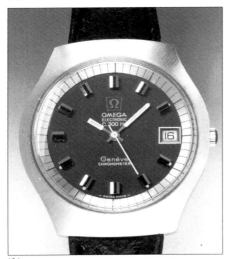

431

432

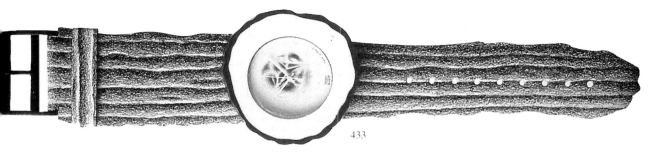

433

Swatches

The youngest member of the watch family is the Swatch, created in 1983 by the SMH firm of Biel. The spontaneous success of the newcomer is made obvious by the fact that within barely ten years, 100 million of them have been sold.

Since the Swatch was conceived as a basically fashion-oriented and comparatively short-lived throw-away product, only a few collectors considered it of any importance at first. But interest grew in the course of time. The real breakthrough took place at a spectacular swatch auction in September 1990, which had exorbitant results. Clever marketing did the rest and made the Swatch into a true collector's item.

The first principle in building up a Swatch collection is to obtain absolutely unused watches. Only these will later sell well. The "Specials" made in limited numbers enjoy particular popularity, as do the variations that differ from models, the chronographs and scubas introduced since 1990, and the models with automatic winding, introduced in 1991.

The prices of Swatches are undergoing comparatively strong fluctuations. For that reason, one should be well informed before purchasing high-priced collectors' items.

SWATCH AS SWATCH CAN

The Great Crisis

Sometimes crises can have positive affects. They can encourage creativity and readiness to strive. They also inspire processes of hindsight and thinking about abilities and successes once at hand.

This was the case in the Swiss watch industry in the 1970s and early 1980s. At that time, it had to struggle through one of the greatest crises of its centuries. Crises of similar dimensions had existed only in the years after 1876 and in the 1930s. In 1876 the World's Fair in Philadelphia led to the so-called "American Crisis", because in the new world Switzerland had to accept the painful awareness that it had nothing, absolutely nothing with which to oppose American precision mass-production. In the thirties, the severe worldwide economic crisis set off by the Wall Street crash in New York, did not spare Switzerland. Unemployment was the daily theme of the watch industry. Production plunged to the bottom.

The crisis of the 1970s, like that of 1876, was created at home. The belief that absolutely nothing could beat the Swiss watches of Elmar Mock and Jacques Müller brought about pride that so often goes before a fall. In the unshakable faith in itself, it overlooked the fact that its competition was not sleeping. The competition, at that time that of the Far East, had been awake for a long time. With the mass-production of inexpensive multi-function quartz watches, it was quite capable of rolling over the European watch industry. In Germany and France, the results have been visible to the present day. While in 1974 there were still 91 million watches and movements exported, this quantity was reduced by 21 million in 1977 and reached a low point with 43 million in 1983. Of a formerly significant share of the world market amounting to 43% (in terms of units), not much was left. Switzerland had to get by with less than 15 percent.

Once again, unemployment was widespread in the centers of the watch industry. A hitherto unknown level of up to 12% impelled many qualified watchmakers to turn their backs on that branch of industry. For many factories there was no choice but to follow the path to bankruptcy court and sell their valuable machines to Oriental manufacturing countries. In the once-proud buildings with diffused northern light, where the watchmakers had practiced their art, stillness set in. The windows afforded a more and more gloomy view, and in some places only the faded "Fabrique d'Horlogerie" lettering on the facade spoke of their onetime fame.

The Breakthrough into New Territory

When one has fallen all the way down, climbing back up is somewhat easier. This saying made its rounds among those responsible for the Swiss watch industry toward the end of the seventies. The luck of the future could not be found in mechanical watchmaking. This had been agreed on by that time. The battle for the tenth of a second could be won only with quartz-regulated watches. The fight for portions of the market demanded reasonably priced models that could be attained only through practical production. Thoughts of status had to give way to a striving for profits that was necessary to survival.

With the Japanese competition at their throats, the remaining Swiss manufacturers gambled everything on one card. Out of the competition for the flattest quartz wristwatch in the world there finally emerged a timepiece that, like no other, was to become the protagonist on the international watch scene: the Swatch.

But the path was steep and rocky. In 1978 the Citizen Watch & Co. of Japan had set the standard with a movement less than one millimeter thick. Complete with case, though, the watch originally measured more than 4 mm in thickness. During the course of 1978, the Japanese watch industry was able to beat its own record, setting one of 2.5 mm for the entire watch. This gave the main Swiss producer of quartz raw movements, the ETA SA of Grenchen, no peace. It set a thickness of less than 2 mm as its goal. Yet with a conventional construction of bottom plate, movement and glassed frame, this was not possible. Only a radical change from the traditional design principles could bring success. Reduction of parts was the goal. Using the bottom plate as the movement plate, the ETA, in 1978-79, set out on the path to several world records. On January 12, 1979 the ASUAG (Allgemeine Schweizerische Uhrenindustrie AG) and the brands of Concord, Eterna and Longines simultaneously introduced to the international press, in several different cities, the world's flattest quartz wristwatch with analog indication. Including its case, its thickness was only 1.98 mm, its width was 24.5 mm, and its height 29.60 mm. One had to pay no less than 12,900 Swiss francs at the concessionaire's table, for example, for the Eterna "Linea I" with a leather strap, this version including a gold case and crocodile band. The version with a gold band cost an impressive 25,800 Swiss francs. The "Feuille d'Or" by Longines or the comparable Concord model was selling at similar prices. A mere government official earned about 2600 German marks at that time. So these timepieces were not intended for every man. Nevertheless, sales success went beyond all expectations. The "Delirium très mince" project of ETA was only the beginning of the extra-thin madness. On June 21, 1979 thicknesses of 1.5 millimeters had already been exceeded. The comparable Eterna "Squelette" was introduced in October 1979 in a limited edition of fifty pieces. The price was 30,000 Swiss francs. In January 1980 a ladies model, only 1.68 mm thick, appeared. This achievement was highly celebrated at the Basel Watch Fair on April 19, 1980. For retail prices in excess of $37,000, fans could share in this success. These watches by Concord, Eterna and Longines, as well as the ultra-flat pendant by Jean Lassale (with a movement height of 1.2 mm hand-wound, or 2.08 mm automatic), were made more for show than for wearing, since they broke down under intense use. Today they, like the models of 1.44, 1.68 and 1.98 mm height, are absolute collectors' items. With these wristwatches the Swiss watch industry had shown that it was still quite capable of the highest achievement and records.

434   The "Delirium" movement.

The "Delirium vulgaris"

The "Delirium tremens", as it was also called in jest, was in truth scarcely suited to be a profit-maker. On the other hand, ample profits were to be brought in by another venture that began in 1979, "Delirium vulgaris" (correct: "Delirium volgare"), the people's delirium. The service pamphlet for this undertaking cited the following points:

- Quartz watch made of plastic,
- Analog hour, minute and second indication by hands,
- Date and weekday indication on dial windows,
- Apparatus for quick correcting of the date indication,
- Setting by conventional winding stem, in three positions,
- Watertight to a depth of 30 meters,
- Easily replaceable battery,
- Battery life longer than three years,
- High degree of reliability,
- High degree of wearing comfort,
- Very robust construction,
- Successful design, allowing many variations,
- Reasonable price (from some 30 francs) for high quality.

The development and production of the Swatch, numbered ESA 500, was based on the extensive experience that had already been gained in the "Delirium" project. As in the Delirium Caliber 999, a conventional design was avoided. Konstantin Theile of the ETA formulated the design principle of the Swatch as follows:

"Regardless of how complicated the model is, the base of the watch case, which is base metal, serves to accept the mountings of the components. The electronic module, or "grid", is first riveted directly onto the base's back. This grid contains the watch's basic functions, the quartz integrated switching link, the battery contacts and the coil connections. The coil and motor are then installed onto this grid, and the motor which carries the watch's gear train. Not only does the motor drive the second gear, it also blocks the wheel train while setting the hands. The motor is also riveted on by ultrasound and then tested for inertia and current consumption. Then another gear and the date disk are held in place with a steel disk. Finally the disk showing the day of the week, dial and hands needs to be mounted. To seal the case, the plastic crystal is attached with a watertight seal, making the watch water resistant."

Thus, as explained by one who knows, is a Swatch assembled. Compared to a traditional analog quartz watch, which consists of 99 individual parts (55 construction components), the Swatch has 51 individual parts (29 components). Because the whole watch is mounted from the top, using a module prepared in advance, the costs can be reduced greatly. The only replaceable part, the battery, is recessed in the bottom of the case. A lid with bayonet clasp guarantees the watertightness of the case.

After a developmental phase that took barely three years, and was done basically under the direction of the plastic engineer Elmar Mock and the watch engineer Jacques Müller (both still valued members of the ETA firm), the ESA Caliber 500, protected by several patents, was ready for series production in 1983. In the first five hand-finished prototypes, which were given to ETA director Ernst Thomke by his two engineers and designer Hans Zaugg as Christmas gifts in 1981, a 100% rate of failure caused the responsible parties many headaches. In the later pre-series models too, up to 70% of the Caliber 500 watches broke down. The quartz Swatch ticked loudly, to be sure, but it did not tick continually.

435 GR 100, 1983 (left)
GR 700, 1983 (right)

Since repairing the finished watch is no longer possible, high standards of quality and regular checking had to, and still have to, be followed in production to keep the failure rate low. Thus the individual components, the module mounted in advance, the assembly and the finished product have to be checked regularly.

The Swatch - A Requirement for Marketing Strategists

Names are often just noise and smoke. For marketing, though, they have a tremendous importance. For that reason, a lot of thinking in Grenchen and New York was devoted to the naming of the plastic watch. The name was supposed to indicate that it was a Swiss product and at the same time was a fashion article that did not replace the conventional classic watch, but was a second watch. The well-chosen name of Swatch indicates both: It stands for S(wiss) Watch as well as for S(econd) Watch. But with this name alone, success could not be guaranteed. The first field tests in Dallas, Texas in Zthe autumn of 1982, carried out on the basis of a joint venture with an American entrepreneur, dampened the original euphoria of ETA considerably. The Swatch was anything but a desired product that customers sought.

Resignation spread. Giving up the whole project and selling it to a competitor even came under consideration. Nicolas Hayek, on the contrary, urged the directors of the SAUAG/SSIH (Société suissé pour l'industrie horlogère SA) group to see it through and establish its own distribution network. His views prevailed. With great advertising expenses and financial support, on March 1, 1983 the first spring-summer assortment was presented in Switzerland through the Solothurn Wirtschaftsförderung, with Ernst Thomke's personal involvement. But it looked more like a gathering of gray mice with a few spots of color than an array of interesting watches.

In press releases, the management of the ASUAG/SSIH group presented the following marketing concept:

"The Swatch goes with an active, uncomplicated life style, whether as a stylish accessory or a functional watch for spare-time activities and sports. We shall always offer only twelve different models and give the highest priority to production designing. Since it is intended as a stylish-sporting accessory, we shall always offer a fall-winter and a spring-summer assortment. In this assortment the style trends of the ready-to-wear and socio-cultural qualities will be considered. The choice of national assortments will be worked out in cooperation with our agents and most important customers."

437 (top), 438 (bottom) Variations and prototypes from the exhibit in Venedig 1991.

In the beginning, the significant distribution partners were not so much the specialty and export trade as the large department stores. In this way, and with a short-term supply policy, discounting was to be eliminated from the start. Even in the Swatch's homeland, success did not meet the expectations of the sales personnel. All the same, the sale of the millionth Swatch could be celebrated as early as January 20, 1984.

When a team of creative artists took on the adaptable watch and raised the Swatch to the level of a "design object", and the sales genius Max Imgruth presented the Swatch in break-dance competitions in the United States late in 1984, moving it into the Yuppie generation, the Swatch was able to reach more and more new markets. The ice was finally broken.

Max Imgruth once stated the formula for the Swatch's success in the words:

"The only thing about the Swatch that does not change is the fact that it always changes."

The Swatch Assortment Structure

Even though the Swatch assortment became more and more inclusive in the course of the years, its structure is still clear: Twice a year, new assortments of the unlimited series come on the market. "Specials" and limited editions are issued irregularly.

The spring-summer assortment of 1983 began exclusively with the men's classic quartz model, some with weekday and date indication.

Men's Quartz Model GN 701
Unlimited $200-250
Men's Quartz Model GG 701
Unlimited $900-1000

As of fall-winter 1983, the ladies' Swatch was added.

Ladies' Quartz Watch Model LB 100
Unlimited $650-850
Ladies' Quartz Model LN 10
Unlimited $850-950

On March 20, 1985, at the Pompidou Center in Paris, the Swatch Art Collection with a model by Kiki Picasso, was shown.

"Kiki Picasso" Specials
Limited $9000-10,000

The fall-winter assortment of 1986 introduced the "Maxi-Swatch" and the "POP-Swatch".

POP-Swatch "Fire Signal" BR 001
Unlimited
Maxi-Swatch "Nautilus" GK 102
Unlimited $150-200

For Christmas in 1988 SMN introduced the "POP-Diva", the first limited "POP-SWATCH-SPECIALS".

In the spring of 1990 the introduction of the Swatch-Chronograph took place.

Swatch-Chrono "Black Friday" SCB 10
Unlimited
Separated dial $500-650
Normal dial $150-175

4843 men's quartz models were awarded a chronometer certificate by the official chronometer testing station in La Chaux-de-Fonds in May 1990.
Swatch-Chronometer "Turbine" GP 104
One-time limited edition (special) $900-1000

In the summer of 1990, the "Scuba 200", watertight to 200 meters, (with quartz movement) appeared on the market in the USA.

Scuba 200 "Merou," SDK 101
Unlimited $900-1000

On August 15, 1990, Swatch founded the "Swatch Collector's Club". Membership is available to everyone.

Collectors' Club Swatch
Issued only to members for one year. $300-350
Collector's Swatch Golden Jolly, GZ 115

On September 24, 1991, the man's Swatch with automatic winding was introduced.

Swatch-Automatic "Blue Matic"
SAN 100
Unlimited $60-100
Swatch-Automatic "Rubin"
SAM 100
Unlimited $60-100
Swatch-Automatic "Black Motion"
SAB 100
Unlimited
Dark dial $150-175
Light dial $60-100

The spring assortment of 1992 introduced the quartz Stop-Watch.

Stop-Watch Unlimited, ca. 60

In the summer of 1992 the Swatch MusiCall came on the market, with quartz movement, and alarm music composed by Jean-Michel Jarre.

"MusiCall" Unlimited, ca. 60

Autumn 1993:
"Beep up" with city alarm. Unlimited.

A Brief Chronology:

July 1978	First plans for "Delirium très mince"
1/12/1979	Presentation of the Delirium type ultra-flat quartz watch by Concord, Eterna and Longines. Height 1.98 mm.
6/21/1979	Introduction of the 1.44 mm Delirium.
10/9/1979	First service manual for the "Delirium vulgare".
3/27/1980	Elmar Mock and Jacques Müller receive permission from Dr. Ernst Thomke to buy a casting machine for 250,000 francs to produce ESA 500 watches.
4/19/1980	Introduction of the world's flattest wristwatch. 0.98 mm thick.
June 1981	The "Delirium vulgare" receives its almost final form and new factory project name "Popularis".
July 1981	The brand name "Swatch" is decided on.
Christmas 1981	Ernst Thomke receives the first five prototypes as a gift from Elmar Mock, Jacques Müller and Hans Zaugg.
12/25/1981	Thomke reports that the watches are not operating.
July 1982	A pre-series of 300,000 Swatches is produced.
Fall 1982	An unsuccessful field test of the Swatch begins in Dallas, Texas.
3/1/1983	The Swatch is made available to the Swiss public in Zürich.
12/8/1983	Merger of ASUAG and SSIH.
1/20/1984	The millionth Swatch is produced.
12/31/1984	3,503,000 Swatches have been produced.
Summer 1985	ASUAG/SSIH becomes SMH; Nicolas Hayek receives 51% of the nominal stock capital of 300 million francs.
Fall 1985	Ten million Swatches have been produced.
9/24/1988	Fifty million Swatches have been produced.
Sept. 1991	729 Swatch models and 290 versions are exhibited in Venice.
Sept. 1992	Festivities in Zermatt to honor the hundred millionth Swatch.
10/4/1993	1:35 PM, introduction of the Automatic Swatch with solid platinum case by Nicolas G. Hayek.

The Swatch and the Collectors' Market

As 1983 arrived and the Swatch came on the market, the classic mechanical wristwatches was an area of collecting that was taken seriously. The idea that the plastic newcomer could rise to become a collectable object was then held by very few. Nicolas Hayek, since September 1985 the majority owner and president of the SMH (Société Suisse de Microélectronique et d'horlogerie) which was formed from the ASUAG/SSIH and under whose roof the Swatch AG, founded on January 1, 1985, exists, said of the loud quartz wonder:

"The news is always the same: Swatch is a provocative watch of the highest quality at a price that everyone can afford. It is stylish and brings much joy."

The Swatch was to be examined and studied so that the assortment, changing twice a year, would always attract customers. Many events in the realms of sports and the arts, as well as events, kept it timely. Nothing more was thought of, in the beginning.

With the introduction of the first "Special" model - a Swatch created by Kiki Picasso - as part of an art show in Paris on March 20, 1985, the ball start rolling. In November 1985 the diamond-studded "Limelight" limited edition was added, and in 1986 the American graffiti artist Keith Haring created four models.

Gradually the Swatch acquired the reputation of being more than just a mass-produced article. When the young Zürich auctioneer Rudolf Mangisch sent up a trial balloon by auctioning several Swatches in December 1989, the world of collectors paid only marginal attention to it. The necessary PR seemed to be lacking. Nine months later, on September 12, 1990, 99 Swatches attracted attention at Sotheby's in Milan. This event, sponsored by Swatch itself, which supplied stocks, caused the great breakthrough.

The report that Gisbert L. Brunner wrote on this subject for the periodical "Uhren" in December 1991, is reproduced below. It reflects the results and the scene at that time:

"The Swatch fever is spreading, has infected more and more people in various countries, and has seen to it that since 1983, the year when production of the first Swatch models began, more than 60 million of these classless plastic timepieces could be sold. They decorate the wrist of the stylish banker just as much as that of the colorful punker. By now they also lie in various safe places, well preserved, since the word has gotten around that the Swatch has a built-in appreciation in value. But this does not apply only to the 'antique' models from the early phase of Grenchen's best-seller, but also to the most recently produced wristwatches, above all when they are of a limited series or at least those of which it is generally reported that they might possibly be or become 'limited.' The most recent example is the new Swatch Chronograph, a few of which appeared in the show-windows and stocks of a few especially successful concessionaires in the summer of 1990. There were six different models that were shown in the first 'I stop very Swatch' catalog with the motto:

'With the "Swatch Chrono" you can let your own time run whenever you want to...Whether classic or crazy: You decide when to stop. Stop it - swatch it.'"

"Skipper", "Sand Storm", "Black Friday", "Skate Bike", "Signal Flag" and "White Horses" are the models that the Swatch collectors look for. There also is a model not shown in the catalog, "Classic Brown", that differs from the "Sand Storm" in having chrome-plated instead of gilded push buttons. For that reason, one can expect a particularly interesting increase in value. There are two versions of the "Black Friday": one with a smooth black dial and one with a divided dial. One can hold the latter up to a light and see two different shades of black. For that reason, this model could become the more desirable one at some time.

Because of the relatively high degree of handwork in comparison with the other Swatch types, the first chronographs were produced only in small numbers. So, many concessionaires had to regularly use the term "sold out". Nevertheless, the gray market served those people who simply had to have the watch - of course at considerably higher prices.

The Swatch Press Agency moved into the chrono-commotion with *"To Swatch or not to Swatch - that is the question,"* for the announcement of the international "Swatch Collectors Club" and the "Golden Jelly" as its membership badge; as well as the "Worldwide Swatch Auction" sponsored by Swatch and held in Milan on September 12, 1990, advertised and conducted by Sotheby's. Here the numerous collectors could buy those watches that they still lacked in order to complete their collection. But the pleasure of ornamenting one's wrist or safe deposit box with a "Keith Haring", "Velvet Underground", "Desert Puff" or even a frightfully normal "McGregor" was not easy to come by, as has been reported ever since.

439. "Silver Star", SCH 102 (left), and "Goldfinger", SCM 100, both of 1991.

This, though, was not the first auction in which Swatches were for sale. On November 11, 1986 Sotheby's had auctioned seven lots of Swatches (125 watches from the 1983 to 1985-86 assortments) in Geneva. The income of 14,685 Swiss francs, including fees, went to the Red Cross, and the watches to the jeweler Bulgari of Rome. Buying just the GB 103 model in 1990 cost some $3000, more than the entire Lot 152 of twelve watches (about $1400), of which the GB 103 was one. In this lot there was also a GB 402, for which the buyers in Milan would have to shell out some $1900. Lot 153 (24 watches) sold for about $2000 and contained, among others, a GA 100 "Don't Be Too Late", for which some $4800 would be paid in Milan. With this increase, the GA 100 was one of the high points of the Milan auction, but these results, as the following table shows, were even exceeded considerably by other models. A noteworthy auction, less noticed by the general public, took place at the Bijouterie Louisdor in Bern on September 14, 1989, with 26 interesting Swatch models sold. Included was a "Royal Puff", of which only 120 specimens, intended as gifts for VIPs, had been made, and which had never been marketed to the public. Originally priced at 500 Swiss francs, the watches went for 3900 francs while a year later in Milan, nothing less that $16,000 would be paid for two "yellow-puffed Desert Puff" watches, both as yet unworn. The same result, namely 3900 francs, was paid in Bern for the "Velvet Underground" model, which went for some $7800 in Milan. The aforementioned "Don't be too late" could be had in Bern for a mere 280 francs, only 20 francs more than the also aforementioned GB 103 model. The "Original Jelly Fish" could be had in Bern for 2800 francs, the Keith Haring "Mille Pattes" for 800 francs, the "Serpent" by the same artist for 950 francs, and his "Blanc sur noir" for 1500 francs. The three Swatches designed under the patronage of the "Fondation Maeght" cost 650 francs apiece, while the models by pol Bury and Valerio Adami went for 650 francs and those by Pierre Alechnisky for 750 francs. The "Rorrim 5" was sold for another 650 francs. The three models by the Belgian artist Jean Michel Folon, which had been sold in 1987 in quantities of 5000 each only in Belgium and Italy for about 100 francs each, brought in 400 francs (No. 1) and 550 francs (No. 2 and 3 each) in Bern.

For the GO 001 "Breakdance", of which a series of 5000 pieces had been produced in 1984 for the World Breakdance Championship at the "Roxy" disco in New York, 1300 francs had been paid in Bern. The GZ 101, of which

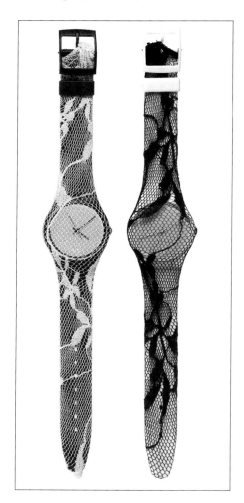

440. "Velvet Underground", GZ 999, series of 500, 1983.

441. "Don't be too late", GA 100, 1984.

442. "Pol Bury", GZ 107, and GZ 111.

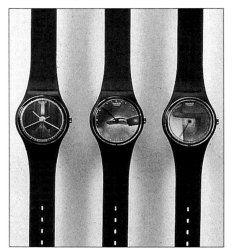

443. Art Collection, 1987.

10,000 were made in the same year for the Olympic Committee on the occasion of the games in Los Angeles, went for 500 francs. The GB 105 "Blackout", an unlimited regular-issue model of 1985, intended more as an accessory than a functioning watch, went for 450 francs, and the "Techno Sphere", likewise a regular issue in 1985, only 150 francs.

In comparison, here are some results of the Milan auction, prices including fees:

Lot	Brief Description/Year	Estimate 1000 Lira	Actual Bid
02	GB 702/1983	450/500	900
05	GN 101/1983	450/500	1,600
07	GB 700/1983	450/500	1,200
09	GW 101/1983 "Tennis Stripes"	450/500	2,000
10	GW 100/1983 "Tennis Grid"	450/500	1,600
14	GB 402/1983	500/600	2,200
18	GO 001/1985 "Breakdance"	600/1000	5,500
19	Blow Your Time Away /Desert Puff/1988	2/3000	19,000
22	GZ 999/1985 "Velvet Underground"	1/3000	9,000
25	GB 705/1985 "Nicholson"	400/500	2,500
26	GJ 700/1985 "Yamaha Racer"	300/500	3,000
27	GZ 400/1984 "Olympia Logo"	200/400	5,000
31	GJ 100/1985 "McGregor"	300/350	1,800
33	GB 105/1985 "Black Out"	500/600	4,500
37	GK 101/1985 "Techno-Sphere"	300/400	1,400
40	LB 110/1985 "Lady Limelight"	700/900	6,000
51	GZ 105/1987 "Bergstrüssli"	700/1000	6,000
52	GZ 108/1987 "Jean Michel Folon No. 3"	700/1000	4,000
53	GZ 103/1986 "Keith Haring-Mille Pattes"	1/2000	3,000
54	GZ 102/1986 "Keith Haring-Serpent"	1/2000	4,200
55	GZ 104/1986 "Keith Haring-Blanc sur noir"	1/2000	4,800
56	GZ 100/1986 "K.H.-Modèle avec Personages"	1/2000	6,500
57	GZ 107/1987 "Tadanori Yokoo - Rorrim 5"	400/600	3,000
58	GZ 111/1988 "Fondation Maeght - V. Adami"	400/600	5,000
59	GZ 110/1988 "same—Pol Bury"	300/600	2,800
60	GZ 401/1988 "same - Pierre Alechinsky"	300/600	3,000
61	GZ 113/1989 "Mimmo Paladino"	3/5000	24,000
62	1984 "Original Jelly Fish"	1500/2500	20,000

It is common knowledge that the Swatch is more than just "a little some-thing" for the wrist. Various Swatch models have advanced almost instantly to the bestseller stage, and Swatch fans are regular questioners of the concessionaires.

The sale of so-called garden-variety watches, the "Swatchetables" of the Parisian artist Alfred Hofkunst, at international vegetable markets in the summer of 1991 did its part in making the name of Swatch familiar to even the most faraway.

The managers of the Swatch house were not as pleased by such popularity as one might think. This development, unexpected by all, especially in Germany, Italy and Switzerland, turned out to have not just good sides. Frustration grew steadily among the collectors and fans when they asked about specific models and were told they were unavailable. Disappointment also grew when desirable models appeared in the concessionaires' show windows with the clear label "not for sale", or with adhesive labels saying, "from a private collection", and could be had only at several times the catalog price. This speculation on the Swatch caused Nicolas G. Hayek to turn to the press on October 4, 1991, with the following words:

"Our consumers, with their purchases of traditional Swatch watches, chronographs, scubas and, for the last few days, automatics, have created a gigantic demand for these models.

444

On the one hand, we are naturally happy about this; but on the other hand, this has resulted in developments that cannot be justified. The run on the Swatch stores is so great in all countries that it has led to disappointment, nervousness and, in isolated cases, insults. That bothers us very much, since Swatch exists to please our customers and not to annoy them.

The SMH, as well as ETA and Swatch, expand their production capacities constantly. Their products are made available to the markets at once. We ask our customers for a little understanding, since we, just like any other industry, can never satisfy the entire demand on the first day - but surely can in the coming months.

At the same time, we have asked our trade partners not to hoard any Swatch watches. We are also very disturbed that certain profit-seeking persons have utilized the great demand for chronographs, for instance, which were introduced in the spring of 1990, to demand exaggerated prices for them. We are trying to produce so much in the next six months that these speculators will be left sitting on their hoards..."

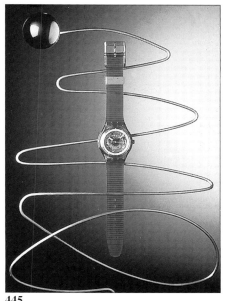

445

Talks with serious Swatch partners showed many to be quite frustrated when the subject of the delivery and sales situation came up. Which of the many original customers and advance orders should they supply with the few arriving watches without offending other customers who had waited just as longingly?

The debut of three mechanical models, the "Rubin", "Blue Matic" and "Black Motion", in Venice on September 24, 1991 also resulted in worldwide enthusiasm. On the stroke of noon on that day, the "Swatch - modelli, varianti, prototipi" opened in the splendor of the Palazzo Ca'Vendramin Calergi on the Grand Canal.

Along with all the production Swatches made up to that time and various Swatch imitations, some 300 prototypes and variations were also to be seen in long showcases. Surprisingly, most of them were owned by private collectors. On the day the exhibition opened, the ticking Swatch was first offered officially for sale in the shops of the city. Only hours later, couriers had taken many of them to foreign countries and offered them for fantastic prices of $500 and more.

As opposed to the electronic Swatch models, the cases of the "Swatch-Matic", watertight to thirty meters, can be opened so the movement can be regulated. Repairing the mechanical Swatch, though, is not considered, even by the manufacturer. The three debut models, lacking the banana-shaped cutout in the plate by the number 12, have meanwhile become very sought-after.

Since that time, the prophecies of Nicolas Hayek have been fulfilled. The Swatch boom has returned from its lonely heights to the solid ground of reality. In the shops, the Swatch assortment, aside from the "Specials", is usually available on the spot. Chronographs and automatics can usually be bought "off the rack" as well.

The collectors' market, with its "antique" Swatches, has also quieted. The advertisements in the newspapers have decreased considerably, and many a speculator who could not cram his coffers full enough now sits on mountains of wares. The markedly competitive climate of 1993 has likewise been a major influence, and no longer does any Swatch change hands for any incredible price.

Normality has set in again. For genuine collectors and fans, the times have never been so favorable for beginning and building their Swatch collections. In the trade for collectors' items and other speculative goods, it is completely normal that prices rise and fall again. The fact that the Swatch, with its variety of models and types, is a thoroughly collectable realm is not changed by the ups and downs.

Tips for the Swatch beginner

1. A used Swatch has considerably less value than an unused one. With a loupe, one can see signs of pressure on the band or scratches on the glass very clearly.

2. Swatches should absolutely be stored without batteries. This protects the irreparable movement and prevents the batteries from running out and decreasing the value.

3. Swatches should be stored in a dark place. Direct sunlight in particular leads to discoloration and changes in the plastic.

4. The original package and the included papers should be preserved. This helps maintain the value.

5. Even a non-stamped guarantee certificate can maintain or even increase the value.

6. Membership in the "Collector's Club" brings - besides the member's special - an annual general catalog of all the models produced to date. Other information also is sent to the members at irregular intervals.

7. Manipulation of the Swatch should be avoided, for this usually does more harm than good. A Swatch should not normally be opened.

8. A specialist can easily polish a scratched glass. Bands are available as replacement parts.

9. At present, a lot of specific literature and price guides are available. These should be consulted in depth beforehand.

10. Swatches are being falsified at present. Therefore one should use caution, especially with sought-after models and special issues.

11. Various Swatch models were or are produced in several series. Collectors' prices vary from one run to another.

12. In many models there are fine nuances that can have a decisive influence in terms of value.

13. Every Swatch bears an identifying mark on its bottom (a number or combined number-and-letter code) from which the date of manufacture can be determined. But the codes are not uniform.

14. The country of original sale is also marked variously in the form of a number on the base.

15. The reference numbers can also be used to determine data about the watch. They indicate first whether it is a lady's or man's watch, a Chrono, a Scuba or whatever. The number also indicates the color, the number of hands, and the presence of weekday or date indication.

16. Note: There are exceptions to every rule! This principle is particularly true of Swatch. Variations are, so to speak, part of the series. They can enhance the value, but they do not have to.

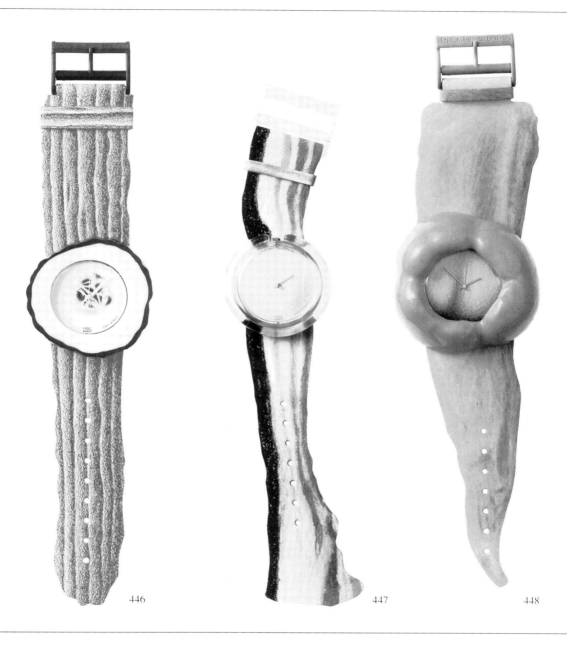

446

447

448

446 Gu(h)rke
PWZ 100 $800-900

447 Bonju(h)r
PWZ 101 $800-900

448 Verdu(h)ra
PWZ 102 $800-900

Swatch-Pop-Specials
"One more Time"
9999 made
by Alfred Hofkunst

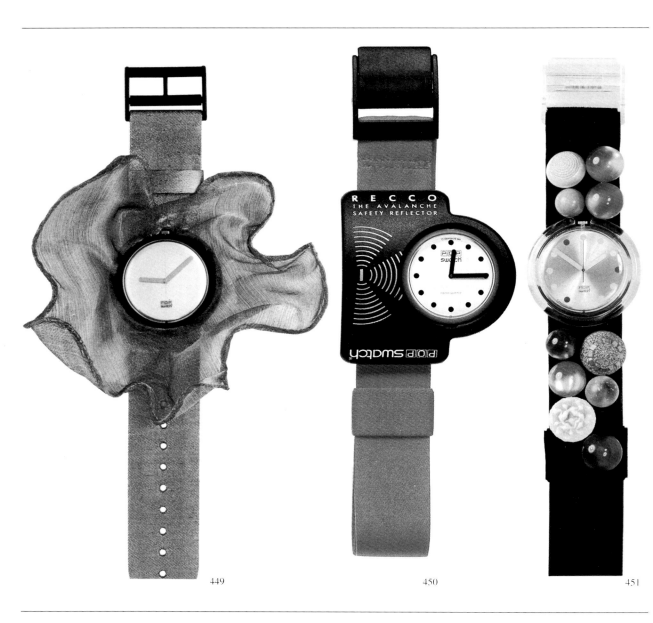

449

450

451

449 Swatch-Pop-Specials
Christmas Specials 1990
Encontador 9999 made
PWB 151 $200-250

450 Pop-Swatch-Collection
Pop-Recco
Fire-Signal
BR 001 $250-300

451 Swatch-Pop-Specials
Christmas-Special 1991
Bottone 14.999 made
PWK 153 $200-250

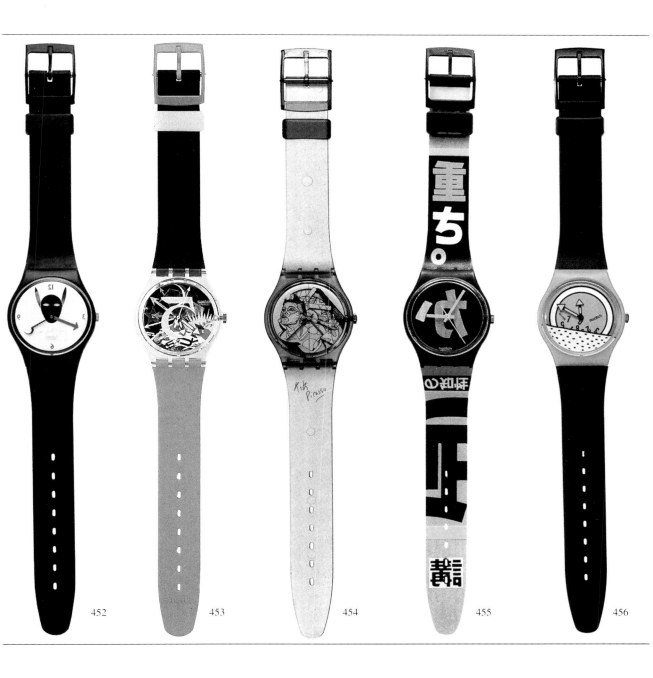

452   453   454   455   456

452 Swatch-Art Mimmo Paladino
GZ 113, 120 made, 1989
$8000-10,000

453 Swatch-Art
Rorrim, 5000 made, 1987
GZ 107 $1300-1500

454 Swatch-Art-Collection
Kiki Picasso, 140 made, 1985
$9000-10,000

455 Swatch-USA-Specials
Breakdance, 9999 made, 1984
GO 001 $1300-1500

456 Maxi-Swatch-Collections 1989
Harajuku
GB 124 $150-200

457   458   459   460   461   462

457 Tennis Stripes
1983
GW 101 $1250-1500

458 High-Tech
1984
GB 002 $300-350

459 Skipper 4 Flags,
1984
GS 100 $1200-1400

460 Fleet Street Inc.
1985
GA 103 $150-200

461 Carlton Pinstripe
1985
GA 102 $150-200

462 Aqua Love Nautilus
1986
GK 102 $150-200

463   464   465   466   467

463 Neo Geo
X-Rated
1987
GB 406 $100-150

464 Rina Scimento
Medici`s
1989
GB 127 $300-350

465 Downtown Runner
Petrodollar
GG 402 $60-100

466 True Stories
Eclipses
1989
GB 128 $150-200

467 Sky Walker
Steel Feathers
GX 406 $60-100

468 Glacon's Gulp
1991
GK 139 $50-100

469 Swatch-Chrono Goldfinger
1991
SCM 100 $200-250

470 Swatch-Chrono Silver-Star
1991
SCN 102 $150-200

471 Swatch Automatic Blue Matic
1991
SAN 100 $60-100

472 Swatch Automatic Rubin
1991
SAM 100 $60-100

473 Black Motion
1991
SAB 100 $60-100

474 Swatch Crono Skipper
1991
SCN 100 $150-200

475 Swatch Crono Sand Storm
1991
SCB 104 $300-400

476 Swatch Crono Black Friday
1991
SCB 100 $150-200

477 Swatch Crono Skate Bike
1991
SCB 105 $300-350

478 Swatch Crono
Signal Flag
1991
SCN 101 $250-300

479 Swatch Crono White Horses
1991
SCW 100 $1000-1200

480   481   482   483   484

480 Color of Money Mark
1991
GM 106 $60-75

481 Swatch Scuba 100 Franco
1991
GG 110 $60-75

482 Christmas à Versailles Bonaparte
1991
GX 107 $700-950

**483 Christmas à Versailles
Pompadour**
1991
GX 106 $200-250

484 Christmas in Vienna Mozart
1991
GZ 114 $200-300

Other Schiffer Titles
www.schifferbooks.com

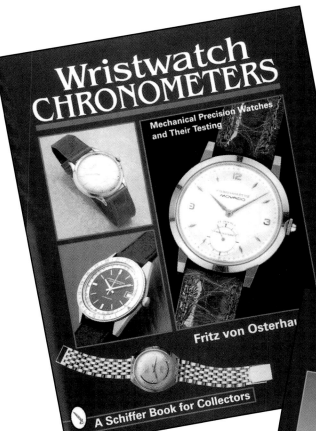

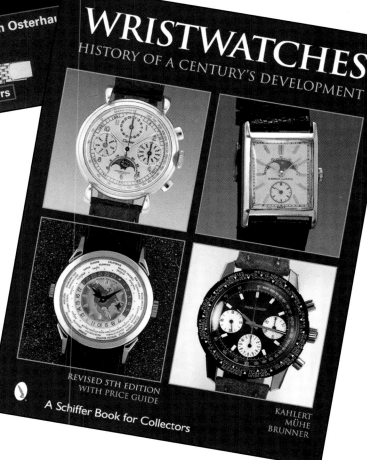

Wristwatch Chronometers Mechanical Precision Watches and Their Testing Fritz von Osterhausen. A richly illustrated, detailed account of wristwatch chronometers and the rigorous testing they must undergo to become certified. Over 400 photos document this crowning achievement of the watchmakers art while information about testing methods, procedures, and guidelines make it clear how great a challenge it has been. A compilation of participating makers based on Swiss Testing Agencies' yearly reports from 1925 and the Swiss Observatories' reports is included as is a guide to current values.

Size: 9" x 12"   414 photos   214 pp.
Price Guide
ISBN: 0-7643-0375-9   hard cover $79.95

Wristwatches History of a Century's Development
Revised 5th Edition. Helmut Kahlert, Richard Muhë, and Gisbert L. Brunner. This respected reference for collectors of wristwatches includes hundreds of watches in nearly 2000 photos, which celebrate both the style and mechanics of the designs. Watches from around the world, their makers, technological changes, construction, and automatic features all are discussed. A current price guide by noted authority Gordon Converse is included.
Size: 9" x 12"   1994 photos & illus.   410 pp.
Revised Price Guide
ISBN; 0-7643-2137-4-0   hard cover $79.95

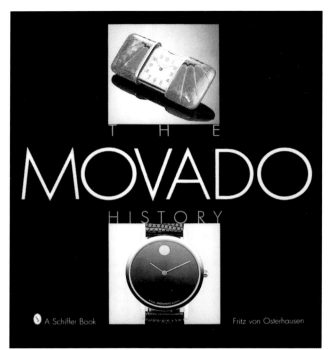

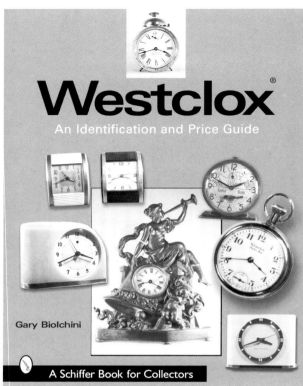

The Movado History Fritz von Osterhausen. A lavishly illustrated history of Movado from its roots in the Jura Mountains in 1881 through more than a century of tradition and technological advancement. Over the years, Movado earned a reputation for pioneering the art of wristwatches, high-precision movements, and watches with complications, as well as water-resistant watches, and their accomplishments are celebrated here in 250 color photos and informative text.

Size: 8 1/2" x 11"   250 color photos   234 pp.
Index
ISBN: 0-7643-0126-8   hard cover $89.95

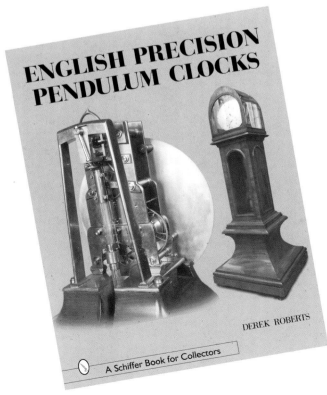

Westclox: An Identification and Price Guide. Gary Biolchini. Westclox was the largest manufacturer of alarm clocks in the world from 1920 to 1980. This wonderful collectors book explores and identifies hundreds of their clocks, pocket watches, and wristwatches all dating from 1885 to 1980. Important information about production dates, styles, colors, shapes, and features original to Westclox is included in the thorough yet concise text. Over 400 clearly-detailed color photographs feature Big Ben, Baby Ben, Key Wound Alarm clocks, Bull's Eye Pocket Watches, early wristwatches and more. This book is essential for anyone wishing to begin - or add to - a vintage timepiece collection. A price guide for all models shown is included in the captions.

Size: 8 1/2" x 11"   488 color photos   192 pp.
Price Guide
ISBN: 0-7643-1835-7   soft cover $34.95

English Precision Pendulum Clocks. Derek Roberts. This beautiful book presents the fascinating developments in precision time keeping in England from 1720 through the 18th and 19th centuries. The work of well-known 18th century horologists, Shelton, Ellicott, Arnold, Cumming, Earnshaw and the Vulliamys, Reid and Hardy and others are included. Their technical advances in precision pendulum clocks are documented along with the evolution of the cases they were housed in, from the early Georgian style to the classic Victorian dome-topped regulators.

Over 700 color and black and white photographs and illustrations document these historically significant time regulators. They have become essential our everyday lives, aiding the industrial revolution, regulating the timetables of trains and being used by clockmakers to regulate the watches and clocks the world had come to rely on.

Size: 9" x 12"   541 color & 214 b/w illustrations   320 pp.
Index
ISBN: 0-7643-1846-2   hard cover $99.95

Comic Character Timepieces Seven Decades of Memories Hy Brown with Nancy Thomas. This delightful book covers the lighter side of horological history. Comic character timepieces from the earliest clocks to the present day quartz wristwatches have delighted children and adults alike, with some of the more creative or popular ones being avidly sought after by collectors. With hundreds of beautiful color photos, this is a celebration of American imagination and artistry. A price guide completes the work.
Size: 9" x 12"   786 color photos   280 pp.
ISBN: 0-88740-426-X   hard cover $79.95

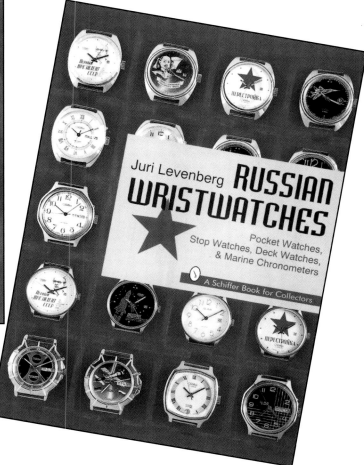

Russian Wristwatches Pocket Watches, Stop Watches, Onboard Clock & Chronometers Juri Levenberg. Photographs of over 500 watches manufactured in Russia and the USSR during the second half of the 20th century, with explanations of their styles, workings, and manufacturers. Poljot, Wostok, and Slava wristwatches are covered, along with a sampling of pocket watches, deck watches, and marine chronometers. Watch faces commemorate all the great moments of Russian and Soviet history.
Size: 7" x 10"   500+ watches   96 pp.
Price Guide
ISBN: 0-88740-873-7   soft cover $19.95

Omega Designs Feast for the Eyes. *Revised 2nd Edition.* Anton Kreuzer. An illustrated description of all the watch movements manufactured by the Omega Watch Co. since the registration of its trademark in 1894. Over 400 watches are shown in 414 photographs. The company has made precision pocket- and wristwatches including the world famous chronometer wristwatch Constellation, the diver's watch Seamaster, and the chronograph wristwatch Speedmaster Professional. Collectors will value the information and the current price guide.
Size: 8 1/2" x 11"   414 photos   224 pp.
Price Guide
ISBN: 978-0-7643-2295-1   hard cover $59.95

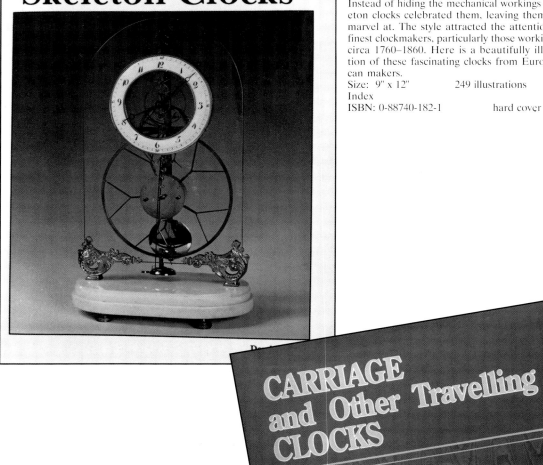

Continental and American Skeleton Clocks

Continental and American Skeleton Clocks Derek Roberts. Instead of hiding the mechanical workings of the clock, skeleton clocks celebrated them, leaving them visible for all to marvel at. The style attracted the attention of some of the finest clockmakers, particularly those working in France from circa 1760–1860. Here is a beautifully illustrated exploration of these fascinating clocks from European and American makers.

Size: 9" x 12"	249 illustrations	288 pp.
Index		
ISBN: 0-88740-182-1	hard cover	$79.95

Carriage and Other Traveling Clocks Derek Roberts. Nearly seven hundred traveling clocks illustrated with beautiful photos are accompanied by explanations of all the major designers' work in this form, beginning from the 17th century. Special chapters present the work of noted clockmakers. The book displays these fantastically stunning works of art and more common popular styles available today.

Size: 9" x 12"	685+ photos	368 pp.
Index		
ISBN: 0-88740-454-5	hard cover	$99.95

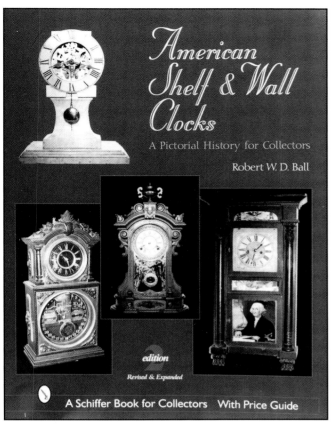

American Shelf and Wall Clocks A Pictorial History for Collectors *Revised & Expanded 2nd Edition* Robert W.D. Ball. Over 1250 American shelf and wall clocks in a variety of forms and designs are each beautifully illustrated and accompanied by an informative text. This historical overview covers the centuries and is an important guide. The up-to-date price guide is useful.

Size: 9" x 12"   1250+ clocks   272 pp.
Revised Price Guide
ISBN: 0-7643-0905-6   hard cover $69.95

Vienna Regulator Clocks Rick Ortenburger. Since their introduction around 1780, Vienna Regulator clocks became a familiar style in homes and public spaces around Europe and the world. Produced in Vienna, Austria, the forms have moved from their early and transitional designs to serpentine, altdeutsch, Baroque, and factory-made types with one-, two-, and three-weight movements. In continuous production until the 1930s, they continue to be popular with collectors and decorators today. A value guide is included.

Size: 8 1/2" x 11"   348 photos   180 pp.
Value Guide/Index
ISBN: 0-88740-224-0   hard cover $39.95

Black Forest Clocks Rick Ortenburger. Over 600 Black Forest clocks are illustrated in this important horological study. Many wonderful cuckoo and singing bird clocks, early glass bell, trumpeter, Jockele, animation, and picture frame clocks all have been made in this region of Germany, where a growing number of skilled clockmakers have practiced their art for 300 years. This book, with its guide to current prices, has been welcomed by collectors around the world.

Szie: 8 1/2" x 11"   600+ photos   300 pp.
Price Guide
ISBN: 0-88740-300-X   hard cover $79.95

Automatic Wristwatches from Switzerland Watches that Wind Themselves Heinz Hampel. The automatic mechanism was a major advance in the history of the wristwatch. The successful design became the hallmark of the skilled Swiss watchmaker as the technology developed in the years from 1926 to 1978. 200 watches are discussed representing all the Swiss manufacturers. Each is illustrated with three photos to show the dial, and the complete and partly disassembled movement. Information on their mechanism and construction is offered along with data needed to locate the watches chronologically and a current price guide.

Size: 9" x 12" 500+ photos 352 pp.
Price Guide
ISBN: 0-88740-609-2 hard cover $79.95

Swiss Wristwatches Chronology of Worldwide Success Gisbert Brunner & Christian Pfeiffer-Belli. An overview of Swiss wristwatch designs in the 20th century with nearly 650 photo illustrations. The many forms and styles of casings, dials, and hands are covered, along with manufacturers' literature, advertising, and catalogs. The firms of Omega, Longines, Tavannes-Cyma, Breitling, Doxa, Universal, Movado, and Zenith are represented, and a price guide makes it a valuable reference for collectors of wristwatches.

Size: 9" x 12" 648 illus. 248 pp.
Price Guide
ISBN: 0-88740-301-8 hard cover $69.95

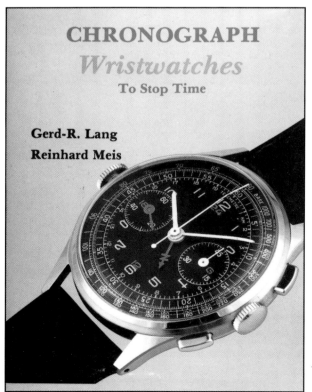

Chronograph Wristwatches To Stop Time Gerd-R. Lang & Reinhard Meis. Hundreds of photographs illustrate this outstanding look at the history, development, and identification of wrist chronographs—mechanical wristwatches that, in addition to their normal clockwork, have a mechanism that allows them to time short-term events. Both the technological and design achievements are explored and celebrated. A price guide is included for collectors.

Size: 9" x 12" 675+ photos & illus. 256 pp.
Price Guide
ISBN: 0-88740-502-9 hard cover $79.95